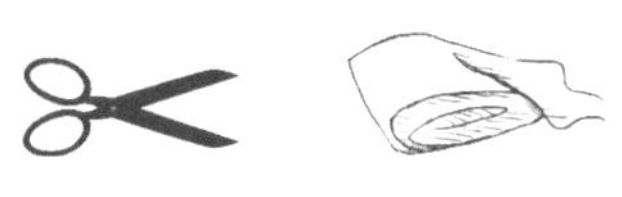
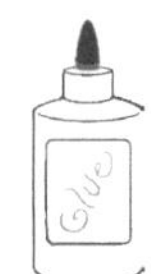
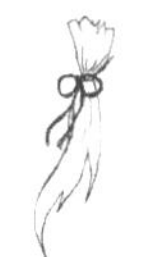
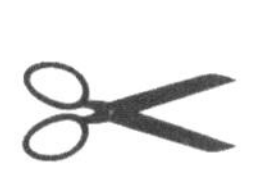

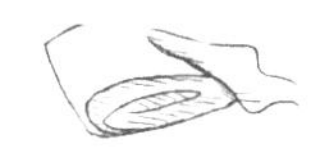

Make Your Own Wigs

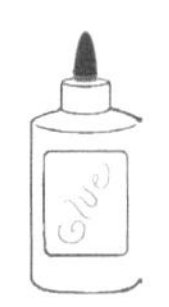

For BJD and Any Other Doll!

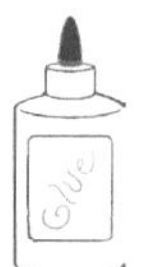

By Jesslyn Carver

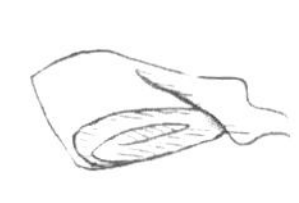
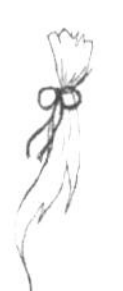
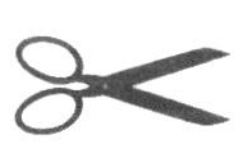
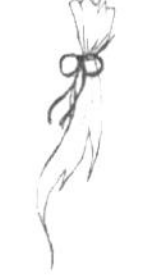
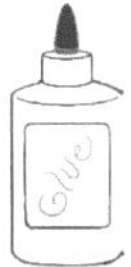
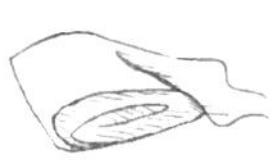
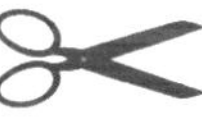

Make Your Own Wigs for BJD and Any Other Doll

ISBN: 978-0-9982104-3-8 (paperback)

ISBN: 978-0-9982104-2-1 (ebook)

Library of Congress Control Number: 2017918663

Dorwik Publishing

Greenbrier, TN

Table of Contents

Introduction

If you are reading this book, it's assumed you've been messing with a doll. I'm with you! It starts simple, you have a doll (whatever kind) and the doll takes your interest in a special way. You're not satisfied just seeing it sitting on the shelf anymore. You took that doll down and started… messing with it. Maybe you made some new clothes, maybe you repainted its face. Maybe you "frankensteined" it together with some foreign materials or doll parts. And you're looking at this book now because lately you've been concerned with its hair.

Hair is very important. The presence of (or lack of) hair makes a huge impact on who we are, our current status, where we came from, where we want to go, what we've seen, who we want to be, our lifestyle, our hygiene, and this list can probably go on for miles so I'll stop there. People care so much about their hair that there is a massive, billion-dollar industry revolving around these… things growing out of our scalps. From uber-rich fashion dudes selling high-end products, to the teenagers on Youtube handing out tips, there are a lot of people, not only concerned about hair, but making money off of us consumers who are concerned about our own. Hair is a big deal.

So why the heck wouldn't we, the doll lovers, be concerned about the hair of our precious dolls? When we mess with dolls, we are trying to find something within them. We want to bring out the best in them, find their true identity, and this can be a lengthy, confusing, and expensive journey.

I, for example, am focused on Asian ball-jointed dolls (BJD) and I don't have to tell my fellow enthusiasts about the long hours spent scrolling the Ebay pages for the perfect doll wig, considering length, color, texture, bangs/no bangs, and compensating with myself, "I can get this wig and boil out those curls," or "I can get *that* wig and trim it to the shape I want." This process is exhausting, mentally draining, and usually expensive. Because there are no doll hobby stores within reach (of me at least) we usually have to buy them online and guess at what they might look like in person or even if it will fit properly. Sometimes we buy several wigs before finding the right one. And after a few rounds in that process, they all start looking the same.

I have to say, I got tired of seeing those same old, brightly-colored synthetic fibers on mass produced wigs. They were stiff, thick, and uncooperative. I needed something a little more personal. Not long later, there arose an online market for handmade wigs made from Alpaca and Angora mohair and they were fabulous. So I tried out these new fiber ideas and found… that my dolls could be whoever they wanted to be now. The natural fibers had the ability to be curled with a curling iron, oiled, gelled, and hair sprayed just like our hair. And they looked more attractive and natural on the dolls because the fibers were much thinner, scaled down to doll size, came in natural colors as well as had the ability to be dyed with human hair or wool fabric dye, and if the imagination is put to use we can even blend different animal hairs for crazy effects.

I also found that this was not a cheap endeavor. If you want cheap, you're better off buying the synthetic wigs online and styling them to your specifications—nothing at all wrong with that. But I prefer the natural animal hair. Please note that obtaining the hair does not hurt the animal. When the hair is long enough, the caretakers simply trims it off and sells it. The hair will be cheaper if you buy it raw (dirty) and more expensive if you buy it already washed and combed. I have you covered if you want to wash it yourself. And then the assembly of the wig will be a bit of work so I hope you like working with your hands. This is why hand-crafted wigs are so expensive: you're paying for materials plus a lot of labor. The effort of making it yourself is worth it. I have been infinitely pleased with the results of my wigs, quality-wise and character-wise. The first wig I made was a little bumbly, I made mistakes, but was able to pick up the pieces, repair the problems here and there, and that first wig was a success. I learned a lot about new materials, thinking outside the box, not giving up, and that I have the power to make ANY character I want.

What to Expect from this Book

I have several different methods to teach you. You can try one or the other, all, and even mix them up! I will tell you about the different fibers I've tried, how to wash raw animal hair, condition it, and dye it. We will organize the hair and plan the wig. Then we will make a wig cap, for which there are a few options; I will try to help you decide which is best for your certain idea. Then we attach the hair, comb it, oil it, style it, and end on a complete wig, ready to go on a doll's head.

What you won't expect to hear about is how to make a "traditional" synthetic wig with a spiraled hair weft. I'm also not an expert stylist and won't include a tutorial on how to make those crazy braids and swirls and twists you might've seen on the net, I'll save that for another book. But I will show you how to comb, part, and trim hair into a presentable shape. I will also not tell you how to re-root a doll's (such as Barbie or Blythe) head—I simply don't do that and am not the person to ask. I'm a wiggy kind of person. We will, however, learn to "root" a wig. If it's a wig you want to make for your Blythe or Barbie then you came to the right place. ALL dolls are welcome!

How to Follow the Tutorial

Each chapter focuses on a task, as each part of making a wig is its own big task. These tasks are Prepping the Hair, Making the Wig Cap, Attaching the Hair, and Finishing Up or Styling. When you begin a task, you will have an option of methods and will have to choose which one interests you and is best for your idea. Along the way I will try my best to offer tips for each method. Whenever I reference a technique available in this book or product of a technique (like a "tulle wig cap") I will emphasize the keywords in **bold** and Capitalized to get your attention. It will be up to you to plan your unique project. Mistakes will probably be made, or you may try one method and then wish you had done the other, but that's learning, isn't it? By the end of your first project, I know you will probably have experienced some frustration, which is normal, but I hope you will power through and by the end look back and realize that it was all worth it. Each time I make a wig, I take one huge step away from being a beginner, and I'm always amazed at what I did. I want you to experience the same magic!

The "My Two Cents" Segments

Normally I would think that an opinionated instructor in a how-to book would be improper. After all, the goal for writing this kind of book is to get to the point, tell the reader what to do, and not waste any page space. But then I have to imagine how you are learning right now. You bought this book, sure, but you're also watching Youtube and reading blogs and asking questions, which no doubt is drawing opinions out of people! You need to hear opinions sometimes. And by now, I have made a number of wigs, each of which has caused me to learn something or gain new opinions. You are 100% free to explore wig making YOUR way, but you might also appreciate hearing how I had trouble and how I fixed it. That's why I've inserted the "My Two Cents" segments into the tutorial. This way you can learn but you can also know my personal take on the matter and then make further judgements for yourself. But keep in mind that I am only one person and my opinion is most likely not gospel. I may not like something but it doesn't mean that someone out there hasn't figured out a better way to use whatever I'm talking about. In my tutorial books, I don't want to just tell you what to do, I want to challenge you to explore and experiment. Now let's get started!

I'll give you the first step now. Dream. And then draw a picture of your doll's hair. Know what it looks like yet? When you do, go buy some hair!

Chapter 1

Hair

Here is a drawing I came up with just to get a feel for what Paju's wig might look like. It may or may not be close to how it actually turned out, but the act of drawing it at least soothed my curiosity and got me warmed up for beginning the project. If you just want a long, straight "nothing special" style, then you can probably bypass the drawing. But if you want to do anything else, be it a special shape or color, draw your idea and then plan out how the process will go. Knowing what the color and texture should look like will help you while shopping for hair. Though shopping could still take a very long time and be very draining. Just hang in there.

Where to find Hair

I don't have much to say about this. I get mine on Etsy.com. Possibly Ebay, but not very often. Etsy has much to choose from as far as sellers, types, lengths, colors, washed/not washed, etc. Etsy is no stranger to doll customization. The sellers most likely will understand what you are about to do with the hair if you happen to start asking them questions. They probably even mess with dolls themselves and will therefore be able to help you choose. It will be easy to find hair that is already washed, conditioned, and combed too, but the price between washed and unwashed is steep, so this is your choice.

Types of hair

The main type of hair this book focuses on is alpaca and angora. On Etsy.com you can also find plant fibers, wool roving, Lincoln longwool, and synthetic too. The texture of animal hair is usually matte, but may become shiny to a degree after washing. I have to give you a small warning, if you buy raw animal hair it may stink and come with a lot of dust and dirt, so please invest in a dust mask for the separation process.

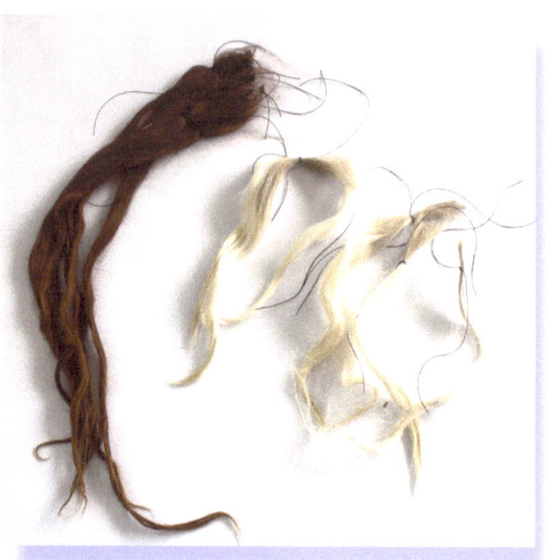

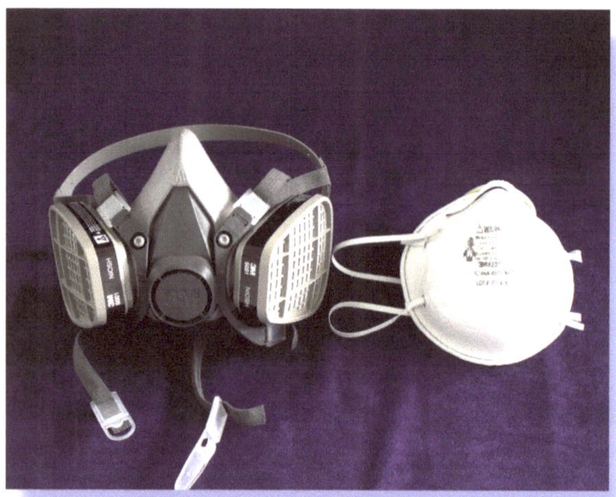

Above: A dust mask or respirator may be greatly appreciated if you chose “raw” or “unwashed” alpaca hair.

Natural or Synthetic? Well natural may come with a lot of prep work before you can begin wig creation, unless you pay extra to have it prepped for you, which a lot of sellers offer. And synthetic is already ready to go. One thing I like about animal hair is its imperfections. It may not all come in exactly the same length and tone, you may get high lights and low lights. Synthetics will usually all be one color, unless you find a color that is mixed, or you can mix it with other tones yourself so your doll's hair won't look so flat—this means buying at least two extra wefts, so keep that in mind.

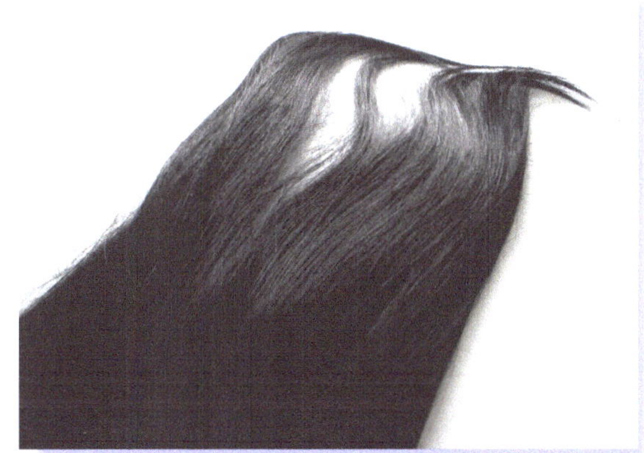

Above: Synthetic "kinekalon" hair.

Animal hair may not be perfectly smooth. It may look good in the photo but feel coarse and frizzy on arrival. This may or may not be a bad thing. When I made a wig for my doll Paju, who is kind of like an old man with long hair, I first bought a bunch of white alpaca hair, and when it arrived, it was too short for my plan—shorter than advertised. I was not upset. I kept the hair for later because I never know when inspiration will strike me and I will jump into a new project that demands that kind of hair. So I got back on Etsy and found another seller who was advertising longer hair than I originally bought. This time I found some that was already washed to save me some time, though it was not conditioned. The seller's cleaning solution had dried out the hair, it was knotty, coarse, and frizzy. Once again, I was not upset because this hair was perfect for my project! It was also blonde rather than the original white which meant I didn't have to dye it. When you buy synthetic hair, it will always be the same color and texture. And by the way, as I worked the hair into a **Rooted** wig, combing and oiling often, the hair came out nice and soft in the end. I also have to mention that if you buy hair that has been washed by the seller, you may still want to condition it with human hair conditioner if the texture is how I described above. You may also have to pick out bits of dead grass that get caught in the hair because the seller won't bother to remove every bit, unless it's the high priced hair that the seller went through great pains to bring to perfection.

Animal hair will not always be the same length. You usually get it in "dreadlocks" that was cut from the animal, each one possessing a bunch of different lengths resulting in tapered ends. You can take advantage of these tapered ends for a natural look for your doll wig. Synthetic hair will be cut from a larger mass and shipped to you, resulting in you having to trim the ends of the wig to get the tapered look… unless you want the cropped look. By the way, you can use heated tools on natural hair but NOT on synthetics. Now let's talk about some individual types of hair.

Alpaca: The type we use comes off of "Suri alpacas." It is fine, long, and soft. It's the longest animal fiber I know of, ranging as long as 12 inches. It can be used for both the **Gluing** and **Rooting** techniques. Will appear as "dreadlocks" or wavy in the online photo, but will loosen and straighten out as you clean it. The texture is usually matte. You can use heated tools on this type.

How much to buy? Alpaca hair is usually measured in ounces (oz.) unless you can get a deal on a load which may go by pounds. I've only made wigs for 1/3 BJD dolls which have heads with 8 and 1/2 inch circumferences. When I first made a wig I bought three ounces, lost a lot of it to combing and cleaning, and was left with 60 thin locks. I only used about 30. By this experience, if you have a doll head at 8 and 1/2 inches then I suggest buying at LEAST 2 ounces. You could lose a lot to cleaning or make a mistake and decide to start again. I think this will always require guess work; just remember it's better to have too much than too little. If your doll is ¼ scale then I think 1 and ½ oz. is a safe bet. If you have a Barbie or something similar in size then you can probably get away with buying only one ounce. Add ounces if your doll is larger than 1/3. Also take into account that longer lengths will weigh more. So if you want to get the longest batch, please consider buying a bit more in quantity. Either way, please don't forget to study the different lengths on the market! Length is usually the deal breaker when buying hair.

Tip: If you attach some hair to a wig cap and then decide to start all over again, you can clip the hair off and recycle the used hair.

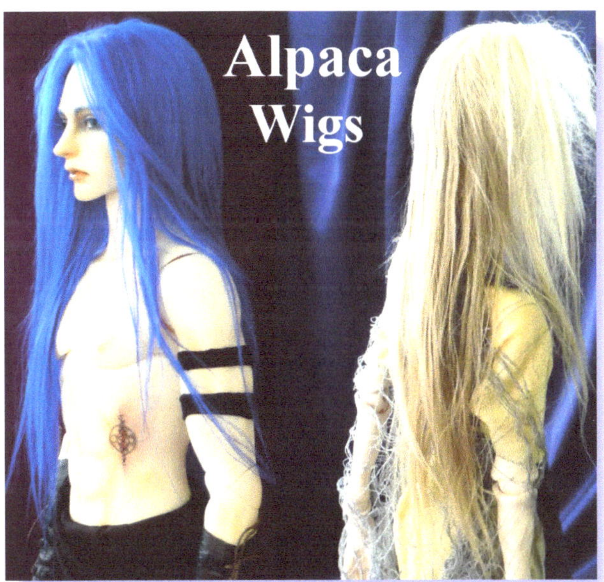

Above: These two alpaca hair samples came from different animals on different ranches. The one on the left was dyed with wool dye, and the one on the right is in its natural color.

Angora Mohair: This comes from a long-haired goat. Ranges usually up to 8 inches, and if you find longer than that, you are lucky! Texture is shiny, especially after washed, and strongly wavy, which may be hard to straighten, so this is a good choice if your character's hair is a bit shorter and wavier. Luxuriously soft! Recommended for the **Gluing** technique due to limited length. Though it is possible to sew the fibers into a **Rooted** wig, this will result in the hair hanging shorter. You can use heated tools on this type.

How much to buy? Once again buy a little more if you need to wash it and a little less if it was already prepped by the seller. 2 ounces for dolls with 8 inch heads, 1 and 1/2 for ¼ scale dolls, and 1 ounce for Barbie dolls. Add ounces if your doll is larger than 1/3 scale. When I bought some it came on a pelt sold in increments of 4x4 inch squares. Having no idea how much I would need, I bought four 4x4 inch squares. It was more than enough for an 8 inch head and I'm glad to have the extra for future wigs.

Tip: If you have a lot of hair left over, and are positive you'll never use it again, then you have a good chance at selling it online, especially if you have enough for a whole wig. There may also be someone out there who wants to buy your leftover hair scraps too.

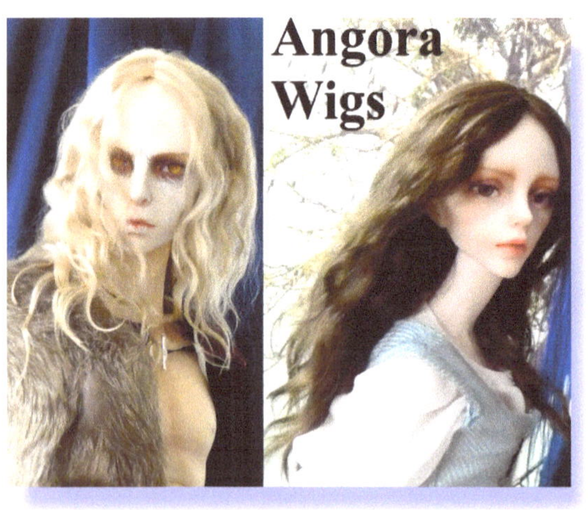

Left: These two angora wigs came from the same batch and were dyed with human hair dye. The waves on the left remain in their natural state and the waves on the right were brushed and ironed in attempt to straighten the hair.

Human Hair: I recommend this type for the **Gluing** technique. If you buy one of those long wefts for wig making at a beauty store then you will be fine as far as amount goes. Ask the clerk if you can open the package and feel the hair before buying because when I bought one, I got home to find the hair was awfully coarse (I bought the cheapest type). Later I made a wig out of 1 ½ ponytails that were cut off of my husband's head when he had it shortened on two different occasions. His hair is smooth and lovely (unlike mine) and turned out to be great for wig making. So if you have a friend who is ready to chop off his/her lovely long hair, be there with a rubber band when they do!

I think style-ability depends on the hair specimen you get as some people have finer hair than others. You can use heated tools on this type.

Tip: If you are making a life-sized wig for a store mannequin or similar, then human hair may be the best option due to the longer lengths available.

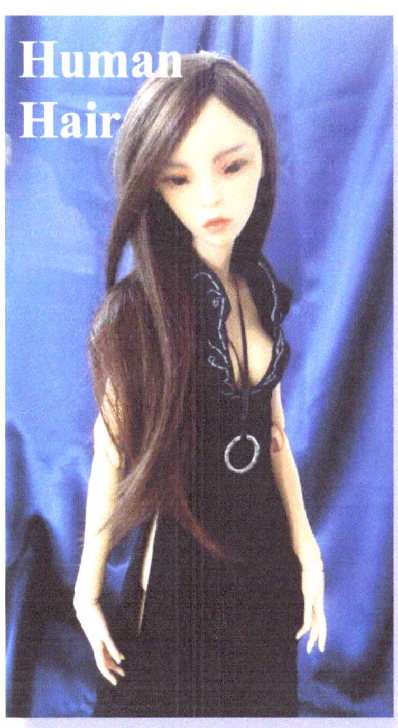

Synthetic Hair: There are a few different types: saran and nylon are popular options. Synthetic fibers are good for the wig **Rooting** technique. People also use this to re-root the scalp of vinyl doll heads, but I don't do that so cannot help you there. Can be straightened and styled with boiling water, DO NOT use heated tools for styling because it will melt the hair. Synthetic hair is made of plastic.

Saran is used to make Barbie doll hair. It's colorful and silky, and you shouldn't have trouble finding your color. Synthetic is affordable. Though does not hold curls very well and is said to fade over time.

Nylon, they say, is shiny but dense in structure resulting in a lack of grace. Comes in many colors.

How much to buy? I haven't made a wig out of this yet, so can't give you advice from my personal experience. If I do buy any, however, I would start by trusting the seller's judgement. Their sites usually state how much is needed to re-root a Barbie doll, so I would start there and figure how much more might be needed to wig a larger doll. I do know that unless you can state the length, some sellers will send it to you in an extreme length (like 18 inches) and you can cut it in half to double your material. This route comes with very good reassurance because synthetic hair is manufactured continually, so if you don't buy enough at first, you can always

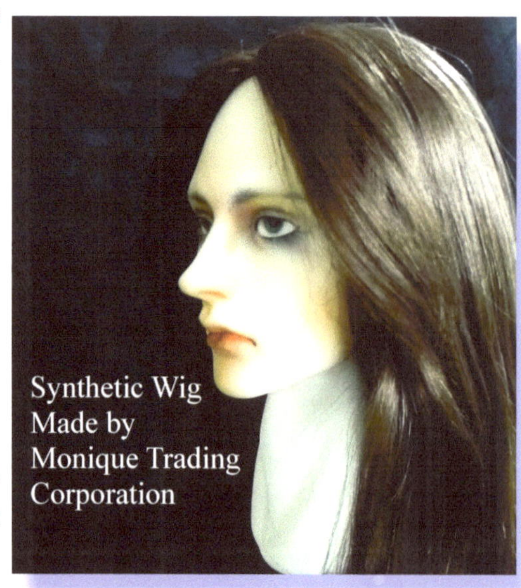
Synthetic Wig Made by Monique Trading Corporation

return later for a perfectly-matching refill.

Tip: If you are making a life-sized wig for a store mannequin or similar, then synthetic hair may be the best option due to the longer lengths available.

That's all I have to say about hair for now. I will let it be up to you to research alternative kinds of hair if these don't satisfy. I know wool roving, which can be acquired in great amounts, can be used, but I don't have much experience with it and also I can't vouch for any other type of hair either. Please use your own discretion. Now let's wash some dirty hair!

Chapter 2

Washing Raw Animal Hair

You will need: Dirty animal hair, spool of thread, comb with big and small sides, dust mask, goggles (optional), two large bowls, laundry detergent (I use Woolite), human hair conditioner (preferably in a pump bottle), and curved tweezers.

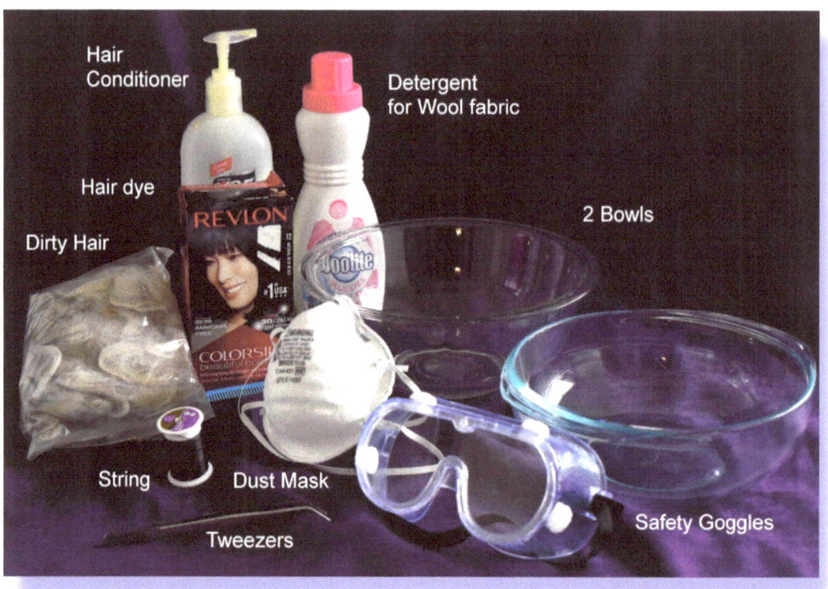

Sorting the Hair

Use this method to clean both dirty alpaca and angora hair. I will be showing Suri Alpaca hair in the examples below. Whether it just arrived in your mailbox, or your rancher-friend let you clip dreadlocks off their goats and alpacas, I'm guess you have a dirty, smelly, tangled mass of hair piled on your table, and maybe you're thinking, "No way."

Yes way—this CAN become a beautiful wig with some time, effort, and love. If you bought already-cleaned-and-conditioned hair, then feel free to skip this section. Otherwise, if your hair has been cleaned but does not seem "beautiful," if it has lots of static, frizz, grass bits, or just does not feel silky, then you can skip the laundry detergent part and go straight to conditioning it with your human hair conditioner.

Now back to that big dirty pile of hair you can't believe you paid money for. Put on some old clothes, or at least clothes that are ready to be washed, an apron if it feels right, rubber gloves if you can't stand dirty hands, a dust mask (recommended), and goggles if you have sensitive eyes. Right now you need a comb, string, and scissors. Also cover your work surface with some kind of paper or plastic for easy cleanup, because the hair is going to drop a lot of loose dirt.

See in the mass of hair all the fine twisted dreadlock tips?

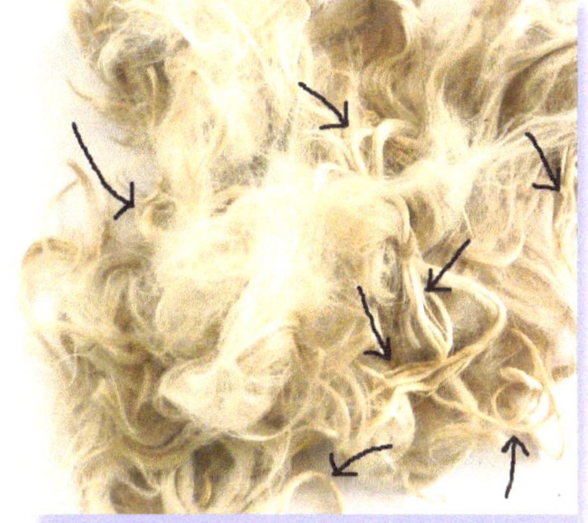

Grab one of the tips, they kind of look like ropes, and gently pull it out of the bunch.

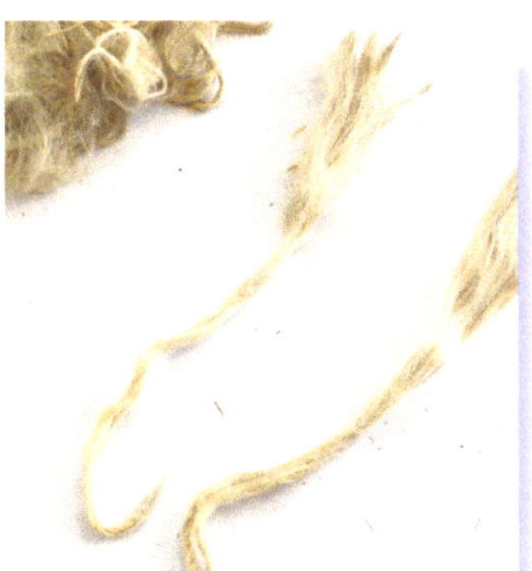

You now have a single dreadlock. The whole bunch is made up of nothing but these (if you ordered Suri alpaca).

See how fluffy the top looks? I find it helpful to grasp the dreadlock firmly right at the base of where it becomes frizzy, and comb the top.

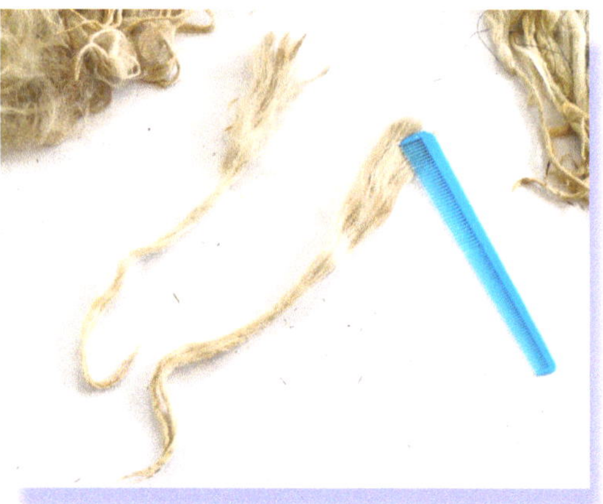

You may notice a lot of hair coming out, that is ok. You are only removing short fluffy stuff that may not have been useful in the wig. What we want to keep is the longer part that is all twisted up at the end. Combing the top should also straighten it in a basic way to make it neater. Now it's time to cut off a short length of string (I do about five or six inches) and use it to tie the top of the hair.

Tip: Go ahead and cut many lengths of string to help you along faster.

Your lock should now look like this:

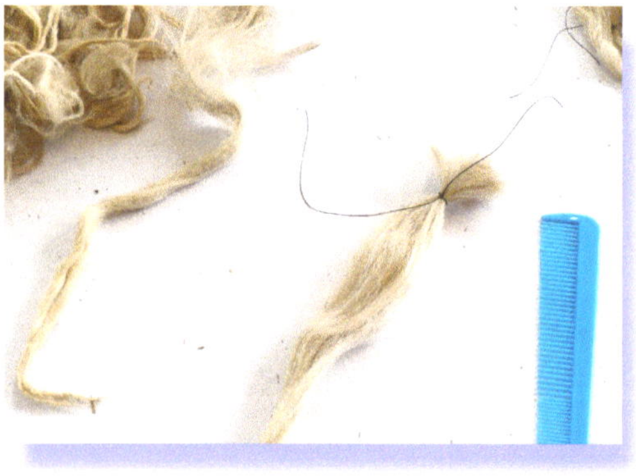

Your string should be as close to the end as you can get without losing any hair from below. Let the tails of your string hang long because you can use them to hold the lock of hair during washing. This could be quite a long process which is why I recommend wearing a dust mask; you don't want to breathe in dirt for an hour or more.

Have a trash can or bag nearby to put the comb refuse in, you will see quite a lot of it. Don't despair that you are losing all that hair you bought, you don't need it for this—you want the longer stuff. Though you don't have to throw it away. You could possibly wash it separately and think of an alternative use for it. Perhaps for: needle felting or wet felting, spinning, stuffing little stuffed animals/ doll-sized pillows, making other kinds of wigs besides what is explained in this book, doll beards(?), attaching to doll clothes for special costume effects, diorama effects, or of course for the **Hair Façade** trick in Chapter 8. Use your imagination, it's a fantastic and NATURAL material!

After a while, you will notice your chaotic pile of hair transforming into a uniform stack of locks. When it has transformed completely, meet me at the kitchen sink.

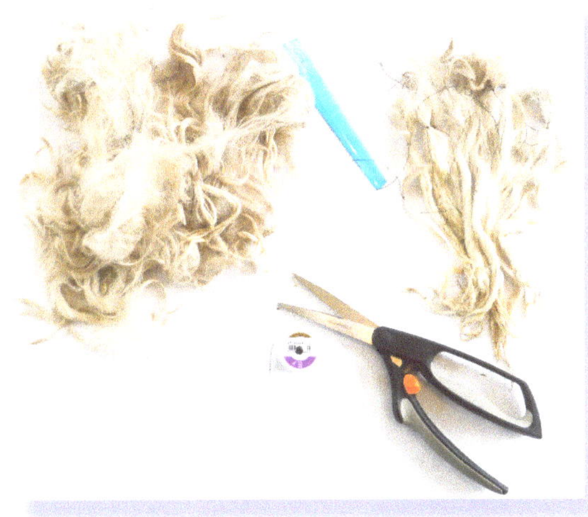

Washing the Hair

Place two bowls in the sink and a bottle of laundry detergent for wool on the counter along with your favorite hair conditioner (I use the one out of my own shower).

Note: I put my conditioner in a pump bottle for ease of access (Not pictured in the photo below).

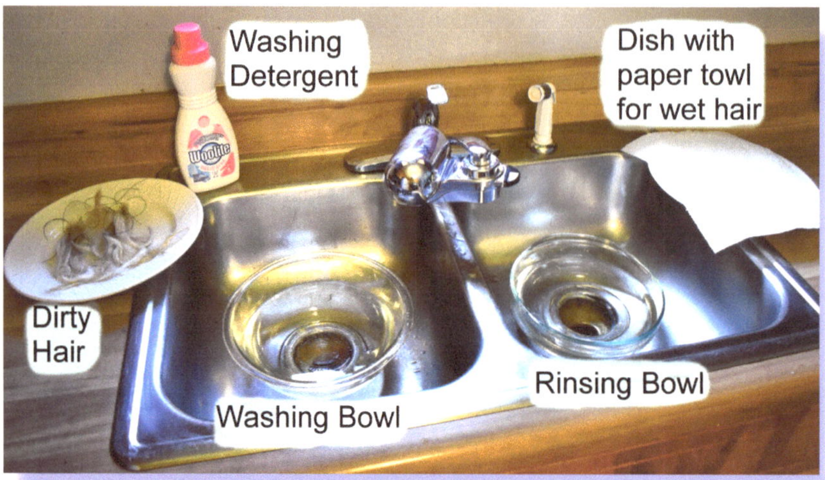

Wearing gloves can be your choice. Also place a dish or tray of dirty hair on the side and another for clean/wet hair on the other side. Pour a dot of laundry detergent into the first bowl along with warm water (not hot) and swish it around to make bubbles. Now take 5-8 locks of hair and put them into the water to soak for about 25 minutes. When you return, the water should look brown and filthy.

Find a lock of hair and then proceed to swish it around in the water—do NOT rub! Do NOT agitate! You don't even have to touch the hair, just grab the top where it is tied and swish it around like it's a little goldfish.

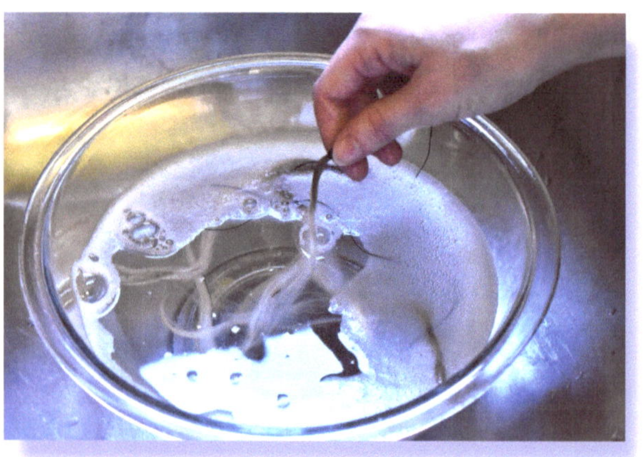

Swish / Don't Scrub

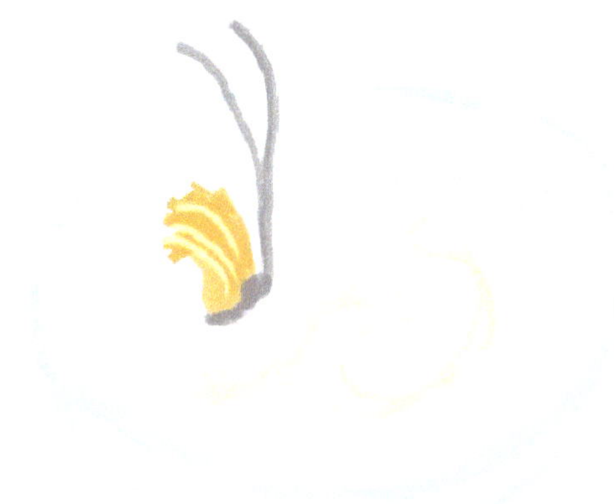

Swishing instead of rubbing is the best way to remove the dirt. Rubbing or agitating the hair will mat it up and possibly "felt" it together. Hot water will also felt the hair together, so please use lukewarm or cool. Swishing is enough to make the dirt and vegetable matter fall out as well, but don't worry if all the vegetable matter doesn't come out and don't try to pick it out either. Later, when the hair has dried, we will pick it out easily with tweezers.

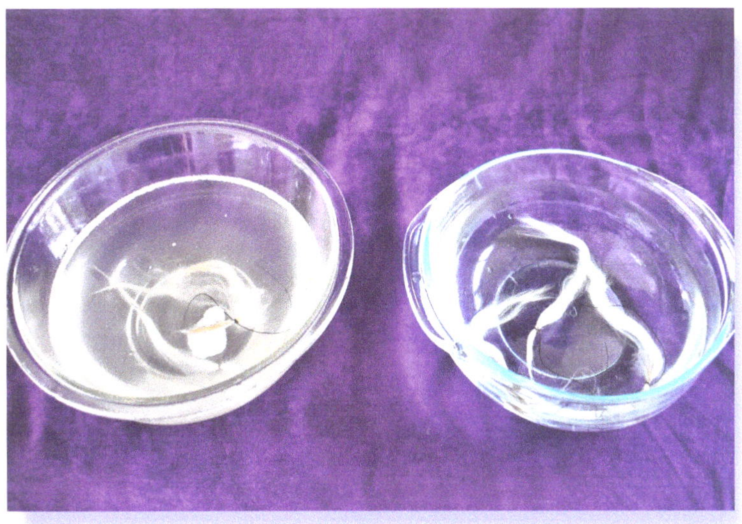

After you have swished the lock for a few good seconds, place it in the next bowl which contains clean water. Just drop it in and let it soak there until its friends are all done getting clean.

When all 5-8 locks in the bowl have been cleaned and are all in bowl 2, dump out the soapy water in bowl 1 and refill it with new soap and water.

Warning: Do not let any hair wash down the drain. It will clog!

Now take all the hair out of bowl 2 and return them to bowl 1. Each group of 5-8 locks gets washed at least twice! Possibly more than twice if a batch is extra dirty. Let them soak for 25 minutes again, swish, and then swish them in the clean water in bowl 2 before placing them back into a refreshed bowl 1 (contains clean water but no detergent) for conditioning. To condition, pump out a bit of conditioner into your hand and slick it down the length of the hair a few times before swishing it in the water.

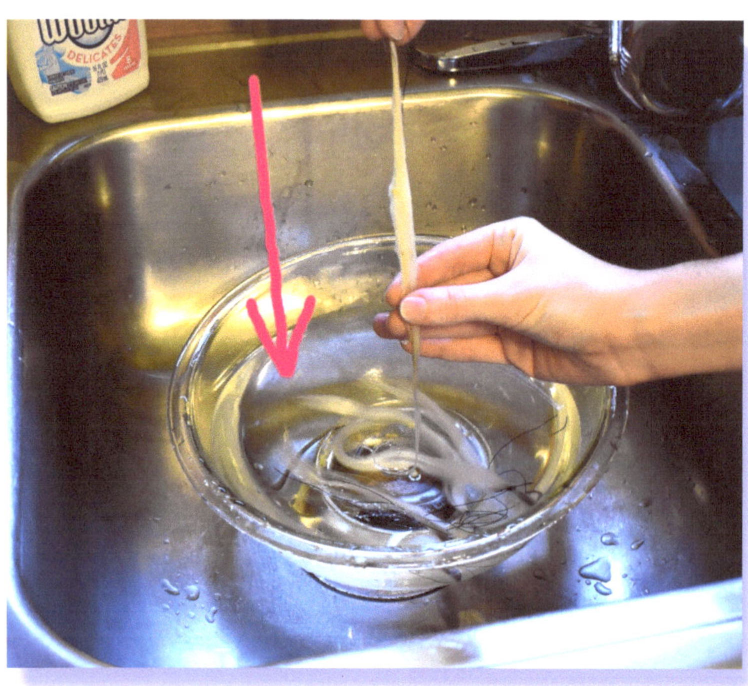

Refill bowl number 2 for one final rinse and then finally place the locks on the final dish to rest before they are transported to somewhere where they can lay flat to dry. I put them in my sunroom atop a large sheet of paper. A window facing east or south will also work great. Let them dry flat overnight, do not blow dry.

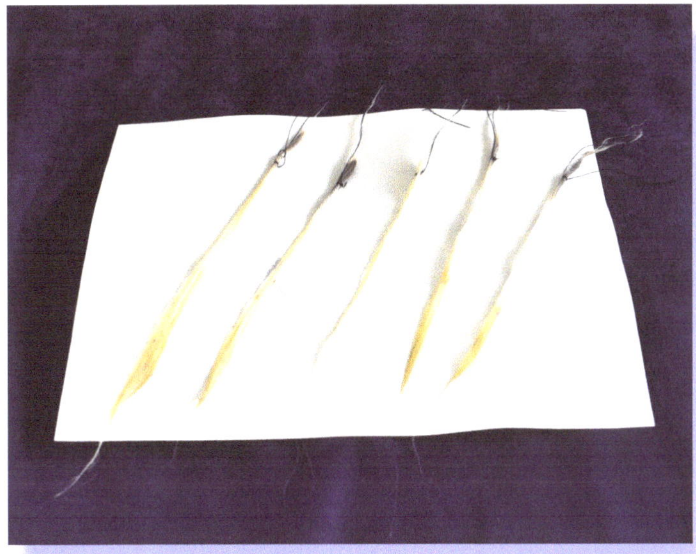

Note: I wholeheartedly recommend conditioning! Why condition? Conditioning the hair will decrease the likelihood of static electricity, causing the hair to be calm and not frizzy. This is what makes the hair easy to comb, shiny, and beautiful.

Let's go over that again.

Step 1: Soak 25 minutes in "detergent bowl #1" then swish and place in "clean bowl #2."

Step 2: Renew bowl #1 and then repeat Step1.

Step 3: Replace water in bowl #1 without detergent. Return locks to bowl #1 for conditioning (slick conditioner down lock without agitation a few times and then swish). Place in bowl #2 to rinse.

Step 4: Lay locks flat to dry overnight.

When the locks have all been washed and are dry, we will comb and pick the vegetable matter out.

Preparing to Comb the Hair

Before we actually start combing, there is one preparatory step to do. Some will choose to skip this step, but I find it helpful to keep from losing unnecessary hair and it also serves to create a sort of hair dispenser especially if you are doing the **Rooting** technique. If you follow my particular method for washing, then you did not remove the string from the locks as they were being washed. As a result, you will find there is still dirt within the lock where the string was. I consider the top inch of hair to be forfeit. I don't bother washing out the remaining dirt, because this part of the hair will be covered in glue.

You will need: wax paper, white glue or liquid latex, a "flat" paint brush that is ok to get messed up, a cup of water if you are using white glue, a paper towel for tidiness, and needle and thread (especially if you are dyeing the hair).

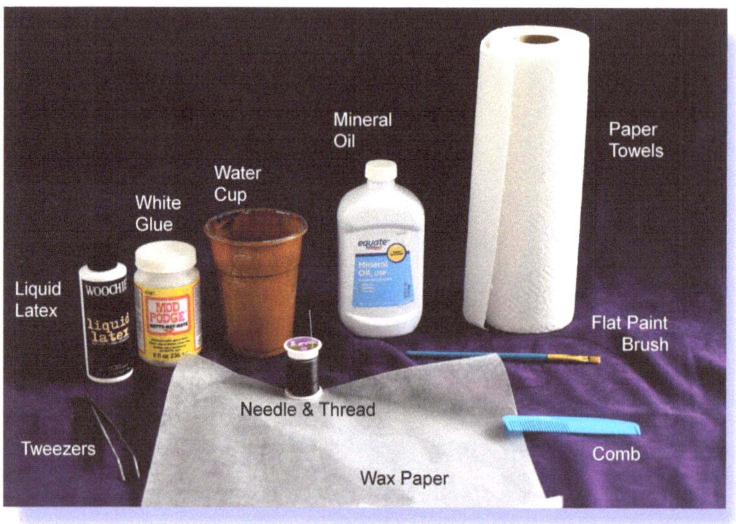

Remove the string bound around each lock of hair. Make sure all of your locks are in decent uniform thicknesses. If some are extra thin, you can group them together, or if they are super thick then you can split them apart.

Take up the first lock and snip a crisp line across the top. This part is probably messed up from excessive handling during washing. I like to keep things neat by snipping it so that the top is cropped and uniform.

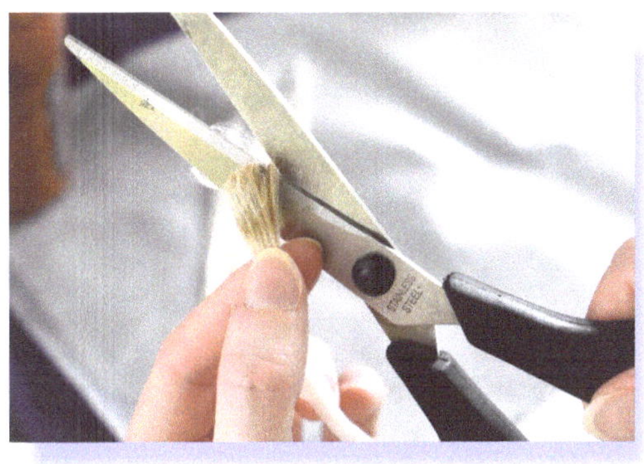

Now lay the lock onto the wax paper, take up your paint brush, dip it in the glue or latex, and then paint the glue onto the cropped top of the hair. Make the glue cover at least the first half-inch of hair, hopefully it will seal in the dirt that was under the string. When you've covered the first side, gently lift the lock off the paper and flip it over to spread glue to the other side. Use the edge of the paintbrush to "stomp" the glue deep into the fibers.

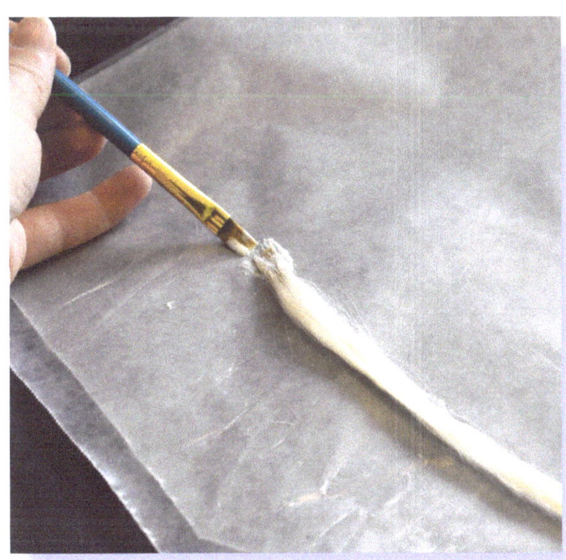

Repeat this process for all of the locks. If you chose to use white glue, wash your brush in the water thoroughly, wipe it on the paper towel, and lay flat to dry so that it can be used again next time.

Note: If you chose liquid latex for this task, you'll notice that the latex will NOT remove from the paint brush bristles. The brush just became a rubber tipped tool which you can keep around to use for whatever craft it would be handy for. You can try to continue to use it for the wig but it may not be very graceful around the tedious parts. Use a brand new paint brush for the small delicate areas of wig creation.

Also note: the dried latex on the bristles demonstrates what a wonderful glue this is for sealing in hair. This is my favorite glue for wig making.

My Two Cents: I used white glue to seal the tops of my locks in order to save my liquid latex supply, but if you want to save yourself some trouble then you can opt to use liquid latex to seal the hair. It will hold much stronger and be waterproof so that you will experience less struggling while washing, conditioning, dyeing, and possibly re-washing the hair locks. After all those steps, I noticed the white glue tends to break down. It does dry out and become hard again, but during the stressful washing period it tends to weaken and threaten to fall apart.

After the glue dries, you can use a sewing needle and small piece of string to pierce the glue right through the thickest centered area. Pull the string through, remove the needle, and then tie the string so you have a loop. This string loop can be helpful for handling the hair through all processes, especially dyeing.

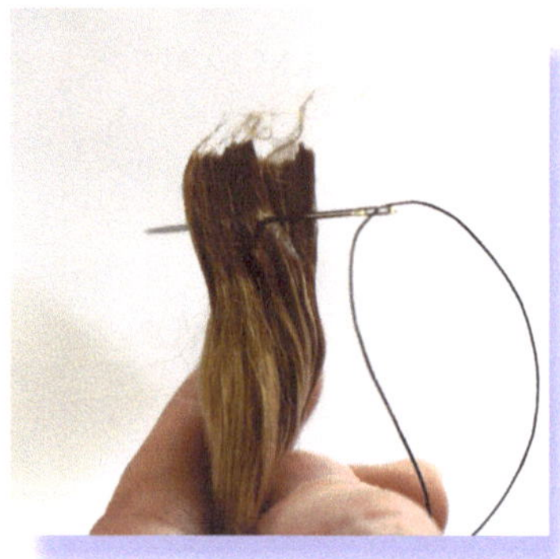

Combing

First prepare a work surface with a large sheet of paper or plastic laid out, or an old table cloth. A lot of dead grass bits will fall out of the hair as you work (all the steps of this process will systematically remove all debris which is why it's good to be patient).

You will need: a comb, tweezers (possibly the angled kind), mineral oil, paper towels (in case of messes), a hair straightening iron (if you have alpaca hair or want to straighten out angora hair), a trash can or bag to put discarded hair into.

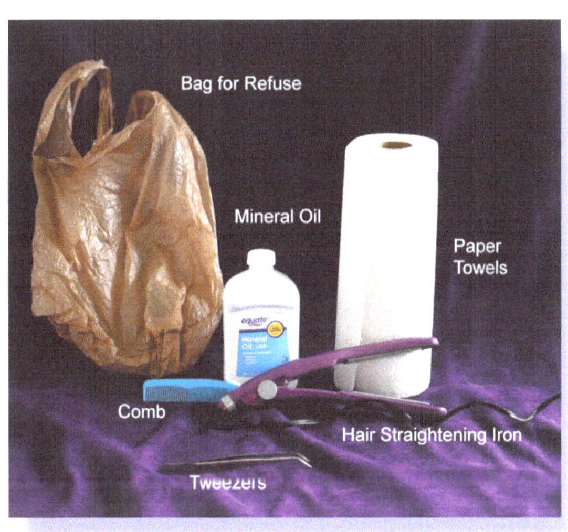

Lay the lock of hair out on the table while grasping the top tightly between your fingers and begin combing with your other hand. I get the most use out of the thick side of the comb, and sometimes change to the thin side depending on the hair's texture. Start at the bottom tips and work up toward the top where you are grasping.

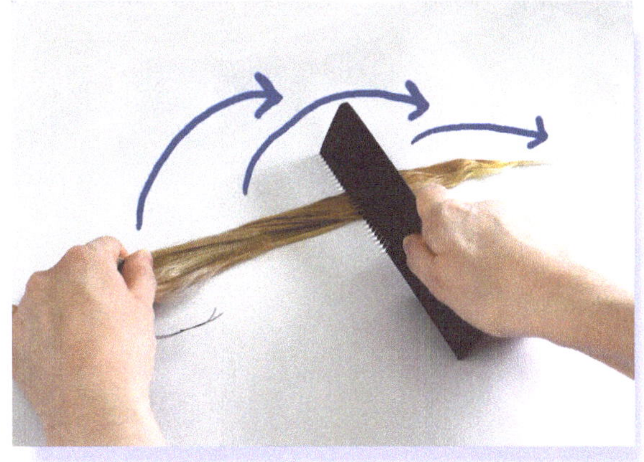

Remember that the hair is very fine and will break easily, so don't force the comb through, though be assertive with it. I like to run the comb through and when I find resistance I flip the comb down and exit the hair, and then repeat vigorously until I've worked through the knots.

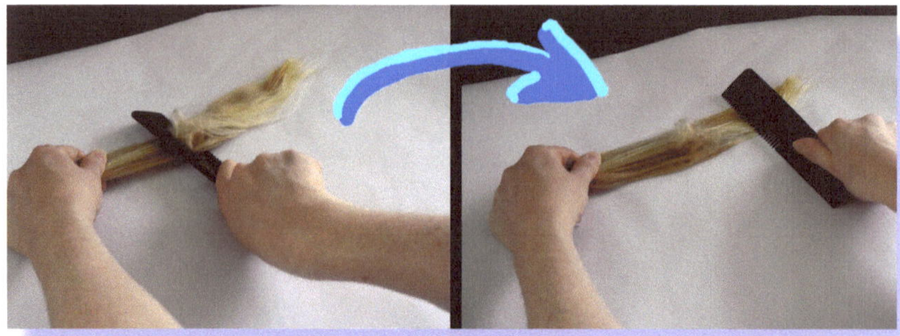

Eventually you will disperse the matted hair into scattered knots. There are a few different ways you can deal with these small, stubborn leftover knots. Either comb over them vigorously until they separate or break away from the hair, or if you have a sewing seam ripper, you can use it to cut through the knot. As you work, you may find a lot of hair falling out or breaking away from the lock. This is ok, the hair that matters will remain, or if you happen to lose a strand that looks useable then you can put it aside to go into the wig later. Even though you are being gentle, you are bound to lose more hair during this process. You will also find lots of debris falling

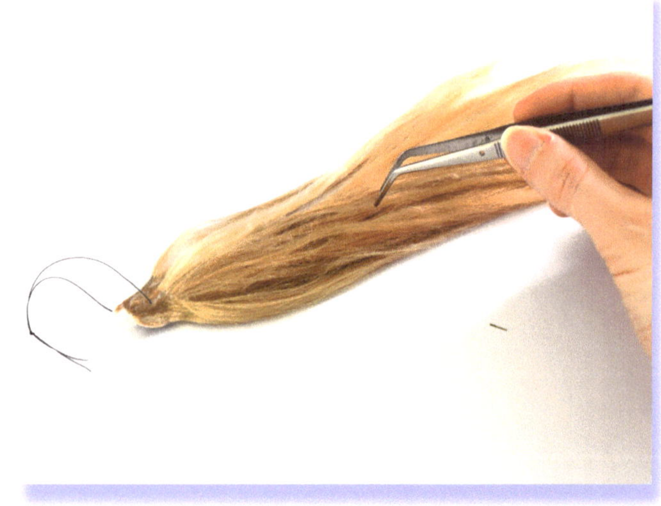

out of the hair as you comb.

Once you've combed through a lock all the way to the top and it seems in good shape for the most part, you can use your tweezers to tediously remove stubborn bits of vegetable matter by hand. Some people will enjoy this and others will loathe it. You can usually hold the hair up to the light to see if any bits still hide in the strands.

Note: If you are doing the **Rooting** wig method, then you may not have to be so tedious about picking tiny debris out of the hair, as during this process we only apply a few hairs at a time. But if you are doing the **Gluing** method, then you need to be as thorough as possible, because you will be working with thicker locks where debris will be easier to miss.

Once you've worked through the knots and picked out the debris, turn on your hair straightening iron, grab your combed lock, I grab two at a time, and slick the iron over the hair a few times. The lock may appear frizzy after combing and this step will remove static and possibly add shine. Hold the lock by the glued top and the string if you threaded one through, be careful not to burn your fingers, but iron the hair as high up on the lock as possible.

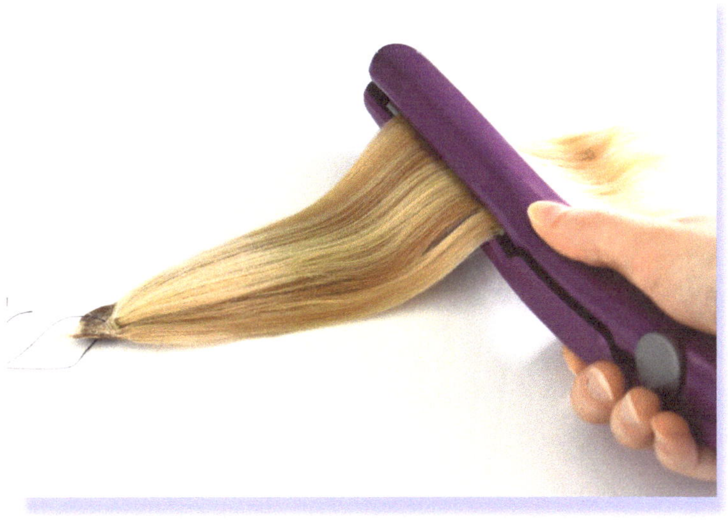

Mineral Oil

This can be used at any time if you feel you need it. I find it better to use during the **Rooting** process to keep the hair neat and pretty. I usually don't use it during the combing step, unless I'm dealing with a particularly bad lock of hair, because the locks are so small the oil could possibly overwhelm it and make the hair greasy which will then require another wash. If you wait until you have a lot of hair **Rooted** or **Glued** into the wig then the oil will not overwhelm it.

The best way to oil the hair evenly is to put some on your fingers and then grease the comb before combing. When doing this you will watch the messy hair transform into fabulous.

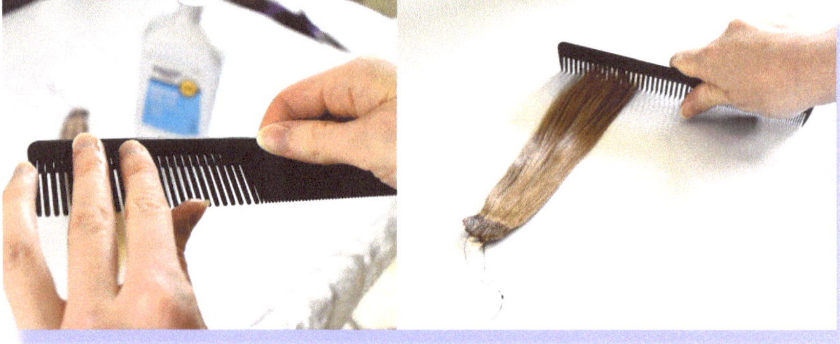

Note: The use of mineral oil is recommended for natural hair only! You can test it on synthetic if you wish, but the natural animal hair is a substance that used to have its own oil until it was washed away, and now adding mineral oil will help the dead hair to stay lustrous.

As you work, you will see a thick pile of dreadlocks transform into a skinnier pile of silky glossy hair. That is the hair that will belong to a doll. Next we will look at our locks and plan the wig design.

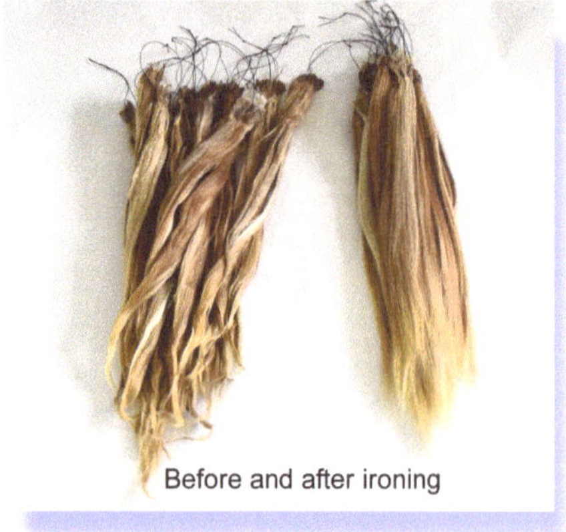

Before and after ironing

Chapter 3

Planning the Wig

Get yourself a notebook and make notes as you read this book. It's a good idea to read the entire book before doing anything, and every true inventor needs a journal. Read and learn each phase of the process and copy down the fundamental steps to your notebook: the washing process, the wig cap making process, etc. Under these categories copy down the supplies needed for each and from that make a shopping list. Since I will explain multiple wig-making routes it will be your chore to choose which ones you will do or if you will mix them up. So go ahead and read this book, decide what your favorite techniques are and map them out in your notebook for a good visual plan. Go ahead and attach your wig expectation drawing(s) to the notebook. It may also be fun to pin your plans to a cork board in order of steps along with your drawings and maybe hair samples matched to clothing samples, photos of your doll, and whatnot.

By now you should have the hair ready to work with. Planning can be as simple as sorting hair or as complex as drawing a picture, dyeing various different colors, and then sorting the different color and length groups.

First let's assume the hair style is "normal," just kind of hanging there, no particular style or

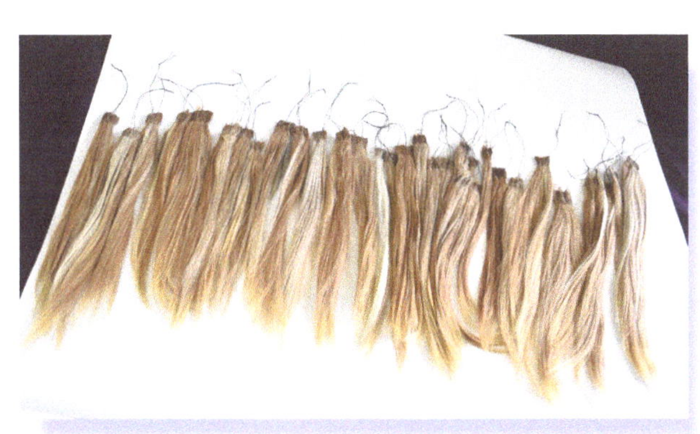

arrangement, just parted at the center or side. In this case you may worry about lengths and if you chose natural animal hair then you will probably have an assortment of lengths. So spread all the locks on the table.

Start picking out the longest and the shortest. When you've found all the extreme longs and shorts, you will be tasked with finding the middle ground and all of its variations. Start with one of the extremes and place them on the table in precise order (I use left-to-right, longest-to-shortest), put the other extreme on the other side in precise order, and then begin sorting out the middle grounds. Continue to sort until you have something that looks like a xylophone. This process will delight some people and annoy others.

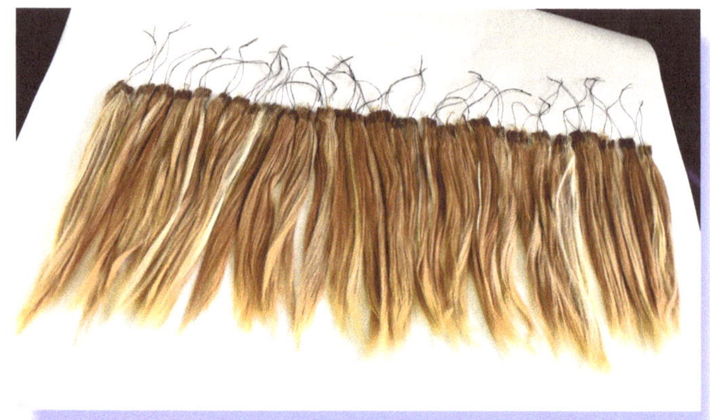

Next I would fashion three (or more if you wish) envelopes out of large paper, folding the paper and stapling or taping them closed. You may also use long boxes if you have them. Divide your three categories, long, medium, and short, and place them into the envelopes for easy storage, remembering to label each one's length category. This will be a good way

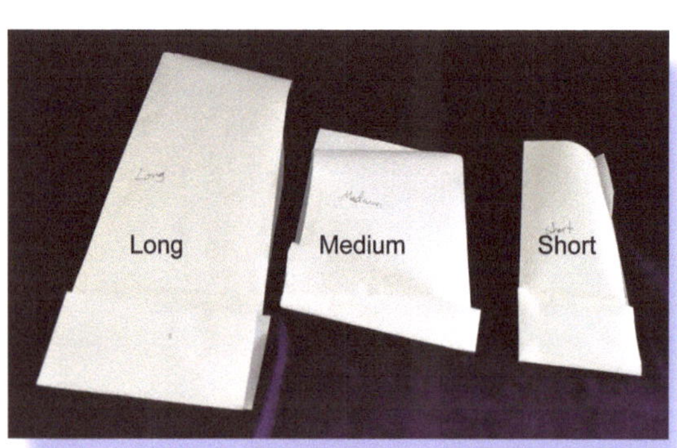

to store the different lengths of hair and avoid confusions and mix ups.

The purpose of dividing the lengths is to plan out the proper time and place to attach each kind of length. In order to get the most out of the length, being limited to what was cut off the animal, you will be placing your longest weft at the center/bottom/back of the wig cap so that it hangs longer and may come to a natural-looking taper when the wig is complete.

As you move up the back of the wig (I always start at the back and move forward), you will add medium lengths at the halfway point and then short lengths at the front and the finished wig will have a layered appearance and possibly long side sweeps or bangs at the front (unless you opt to use long lengths all around which is possible if you have enough hair in your "long" category).

Division is also good for color planning. If you are not going to dye the hair but use the natural variations it may come with, then you will have to separate those colors and decide where on the head they go.

When dyeing the hair, you may have to be conscientious about saving the length. So you will need to pick out the longest locks and color them according to your plan. In the examples below, I drew out what I think Paju's hair might look like. I was aware that my

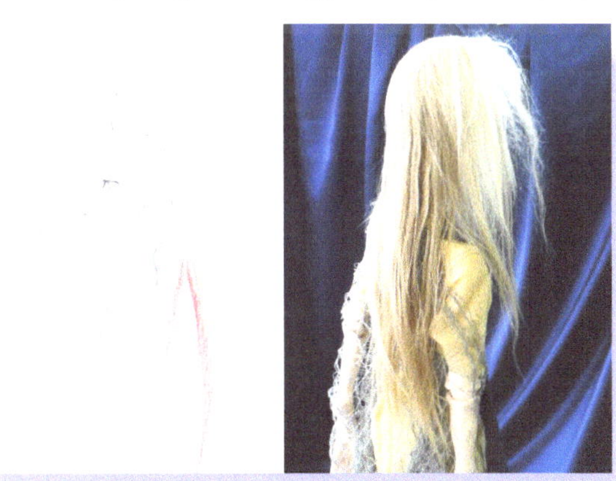

Above: Paju's wig planned and executed.

colored pencil would not show the exact color scheme, but I did know that the hair I purchased had lights and darks. The longer locks were darker and I embraced the color shift and even added shorter whiter hair from a different alpaca to the very front and sprinkled in some Lincoln Longwool hair to create a controlled frizz. In the end, the wig did turn out how I intended and assumed.

Planning also means deciding which kind of wig techniques to use or mix and match. Do you want to be able to style the hair from any angle? Ponytail? Side braids? Pigtails? Then I recommend using the **Rooting** technique which acts as if the hair is growing out of the wig cap. In this technique you will have the freedom to change your mind as to where the hair is parted or go crazy with different styling ideas.

Do you just want the hair to hang natural and you know just where the part should be? Then you may prefer the quicker **Gluing** technique.

You may also want to be really crazy with it and try a Mohawk or shaved side, in which case you will be flocking some of the hair. You will want to draw out your design and decide exactly where the flocking will be, where the hair will be, what the hairline looks like, color location, etc.

One of the biggest aspects to being an artist is to plan, invent, and problem solve. It's really exciting to have an idea different from other peoples' ideas and actually take the steps to make it happen. In doll customization, we can enjoy this to the fullest. There won't always be a tutorial to help you through what you want to do. *You* might be the tutorial author someday! So I want you to explore. Learn about tools, mediums, and products. If there is an image in your head, I promise there is also a solution out there to make it happen. Think inventively and always remember the old saying,

"There's more than one way to skin a cat." If your first wig invention is wrong, just start brainstorming new ways to execute the idea. Don't be discouraged by failure, obstacles are good for the brain. Failure is good.

Chapter 4

Dyeing the Hair

This step is recommended for natural hair only. There are some people out there who have managed to dye synthetic hair using various products like artist ink mixed with alcohol, but I have not experienced notable success with this. There may also be dye products available out there for modern clothing made with synthetic fibers, but success with wigs may still vary, so I will leave that for you to explore. Now let's talk about dyeing natural hair.

I will cover two kinds of dye, one used for wool fabrics, and one used for human hair. Both of these types will work on natural animal hair.

Fabric Dye

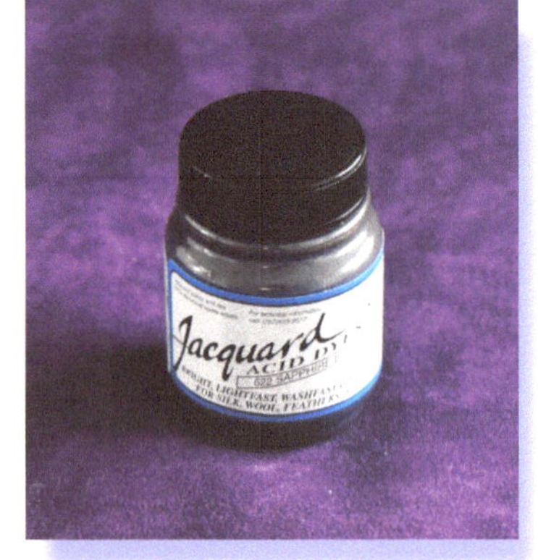

Fabric dye for wools requires you to heat some water to near boiling and then add the powdered or liquid chemical to the water. I can't give any advice as to how to choose colors from online catalogues, this part requires guessing. Just make sure to do only one lock first as a test sample (your least favorite lock), let it dry, comb it out and see how you like the color. If the result is not to your liking, don't despair, just buy another color option and keep this color and the dyed lock just in case it will be useful for a future project.

Warning: Don't let the dye stain your work area! Protect your surfaces well with plastic, and have paper towels nearby for quick cleanup.

Start by boiling water in a pot or electric tea kettle (my favorite).

Place a teaspoon of the dye into a bowl, I use a glass bowl in my kitchen sink, and fill a second bowl with clean water next to it, just like we did when we washed the hair.

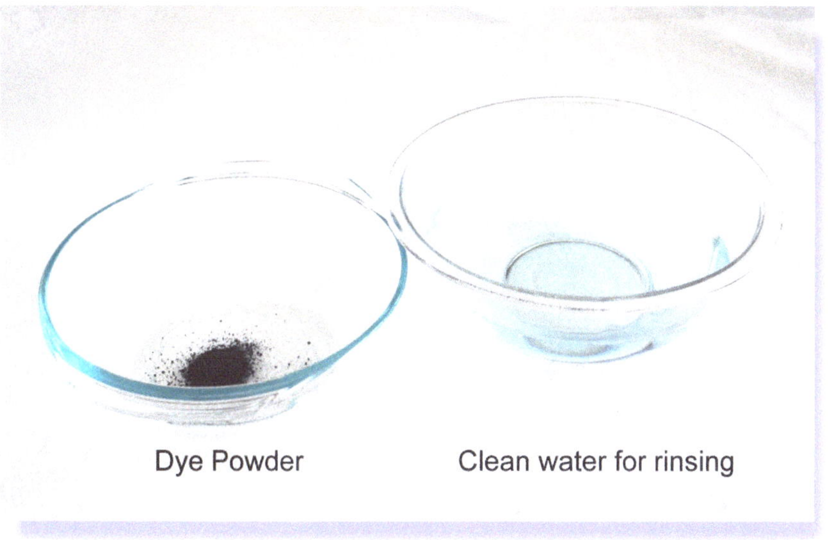

Remember to pierce string into the glued part of the hair locks, as you will use the string to handle each lock. This was covered in Chapter 2.

When the water boils, turn off the heat and let it sit for about a minute, we want it to be hot but not quite boiling. Now pour some of the hot water into the bowl with the dye. Read the directions and use the proper measurements, this may require pouring the hot water into a measuring cup first and then into the bowl. Use a metal spoon to stir the dye around for a few seconds to make sure it is evenly mixed.

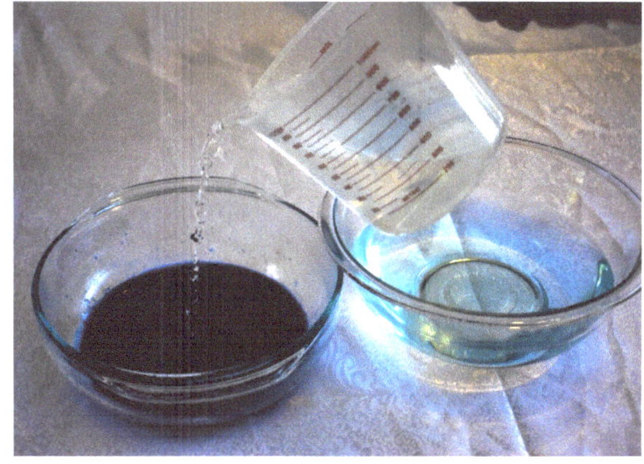

Now the next step is a process:

You'll want to do only a few locks at a time. Twelve is plenty to juggle. Time is sensitive for this process. The longer the hair sits in the hot dye bowl, the darker it will come out. Once you've placed the first lock in, it will have been there for a few seconds as you fumble to grab the second lock and place it in. You may be fighting with air bubbles trapped in the hair. You don't want the hair to float at the top of the liquid, you want it so sink and soak up dye as evenly as possible. So wear thick gloves and try to pinch the bubbles out of the locks.

Think of your bowl of dye as a clock. Imagine twelve o' clock at the top, one o'clock next to that and so on.

Place lock 1 at the twelve o'clock position (or one o' clock if you prefer), let its string stick out of the bowl for ease of access. And then continue to place the locks at the rest of the clock positions until you have enough to work with. We are naming the positions because we want to take them out in the same order we put them in, this will help to make sure that none of the locks miss out on immersion time.

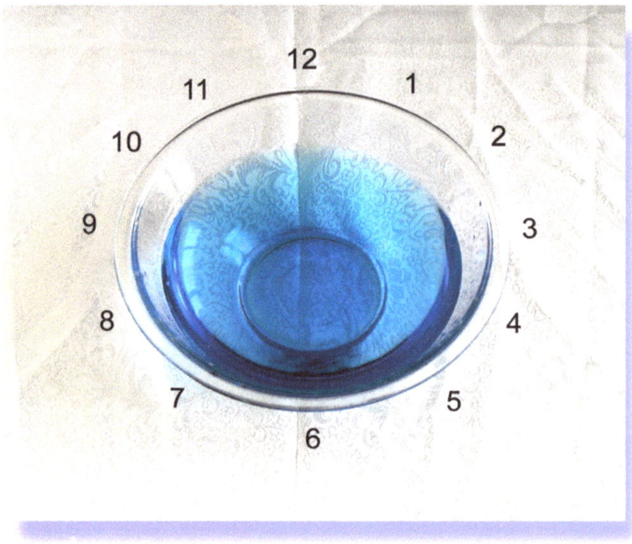

Tip: If you are going for an ombré look for your wig, you can manipulate the times the different groups of hair are immersed. Take some out early for lighter values and leave others in longer for darker values.

When all the locks are in, set a timer for 30 minutes, or whichever you feel is best for the color value you are looking for. If you practiced beforehand, you may already have an idea as to how long the color sits in the dye. When the timer is finished, lift lock 1 out of the dye, use a gloved hand to slick the excess dye out of the hair, and then place it in the second bowl filled with clean water. Continue in the order in which you placed the hair.

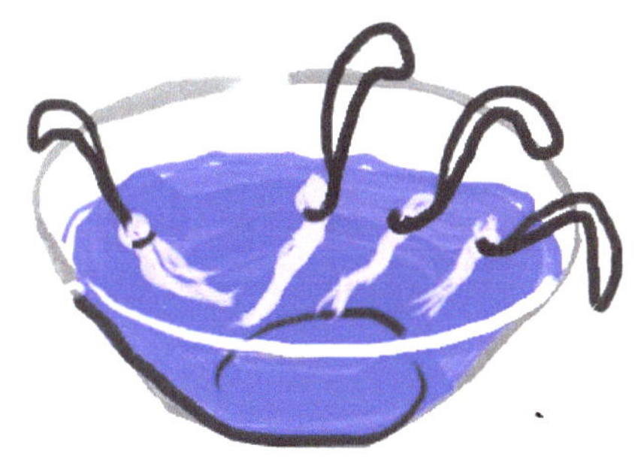

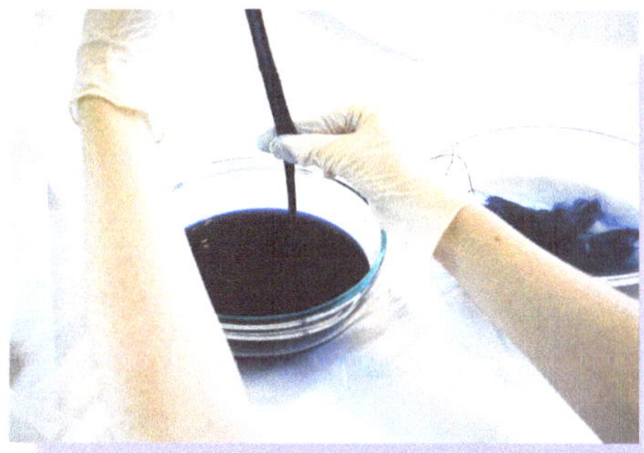

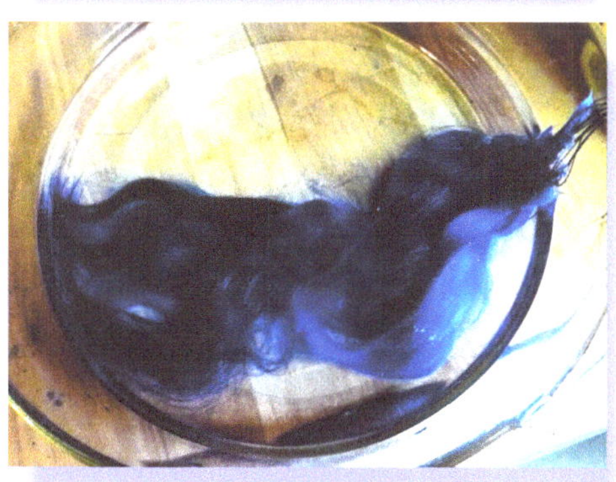

Above: Dyed hair chilling in cold water.

Now we are going to try to rinse all the dye out that we can so it does not stain the doll when made into a wig. Use COLD water to rinse the dyed hair several times, and then place ice cubes into the water for the hair to soak in. Let the hair soak for 25 minutes each time until the water no longer changes color. This could take several sessions.

When the dye process is complete, let the

locks lay out flat to dry overnight like they did before. The next day, comb them again to see how they look.

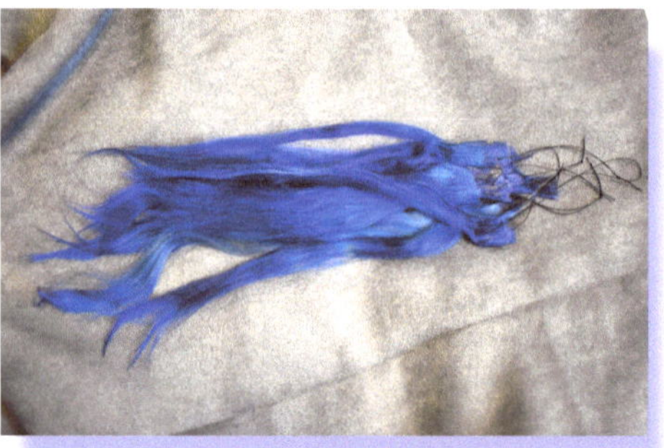

Human hair dye

There are a number of different ways to use dye for human hair. The angora hair I bought came on a pelt and I decided it was best to leave the hair on the skin for the dyeing part. First I covered the work area in protective plastic and then secured my pelt square (or hair locks) to a regular clipboard to keep it steady. You can also tape the locks (over the glued tops) down to a board.

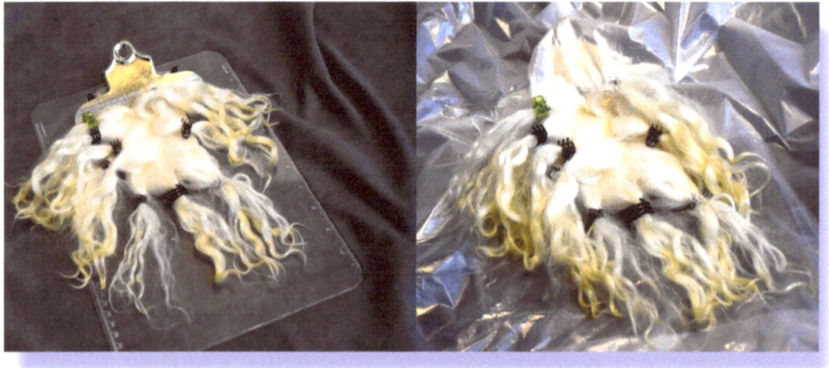

Above: When using human hair dye, I like to secure the hair to a clipboard. The photo at above-right shows the clipboard working from beneath a large sheet of plastic for tidiness. The white angora hair is attached to a pelt and has clips sectioning it off as if I'm working on a human head. The red angora hair (top of next page) is in glued locks.

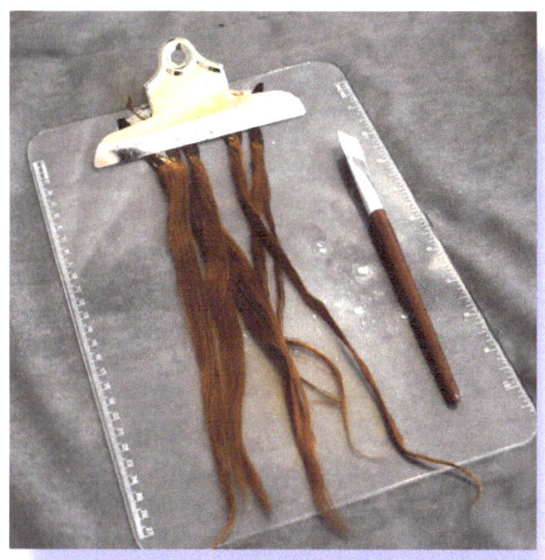

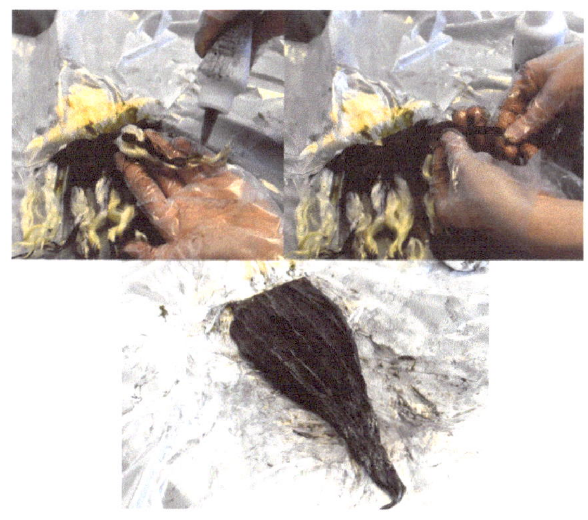

I treated it like dyeing a person's hair, first sectioning off the hair into little ponytails with butterfly clips (on the pelt). Mix up your dye as the manufacturer instructs, wear gloves, and then squirt the dye onto the roots of the pelt and massage gently with your fingers. When the entire root area is covered, remove the clips and apply the dye mixture to the ponytails and slick your hands down the length of each. Do not agitate or tease the hair, instead try to make the hair spread apart by pressing firmly with your fingers to make sure the dye seeps all the way through. When you feel the ponytails are all saturated, you can stop. Do not feel obligated to use the entire bottle of dye on this little bit of hair. Let the hair set for up to an hour, remembering that the longer you leave it in, the darker it will be.

Note: If your alpaca/angora hair is white, you may need to leave the dye in for the max amount of time the instructions call for, if you want the hair to come out the richest, darkest shade of the color. White angora hair tends to be a beautiful pearly color and when I dyed it in “medium brown” dye, it came out a beautiful pearly ash blonde. Too bad my doll character called for dark mahogany brown. I went back to the store, bought “dark brown,” and re-dyed the hair.

After the allotted amount of time has gone by, you will rinse the hair out thoroughly until the water rinses clean, and then use the conditioner that comes with the dye.

An alternative way to dye the hair is to use a firm flat paintbrush. This is best for when you want to dye one lock of hair in multiple colors or dye only the tips for an ombré appearance. Simply use the paintbrush to dab where you want the color to be and let sit for the suggested amount of time and then rinse.

And now that you’ve dyed the hair in the color that pleases your doll, you will want to go through another combing session to make it look fabulous, and then we’ll go on to make the wig cap.

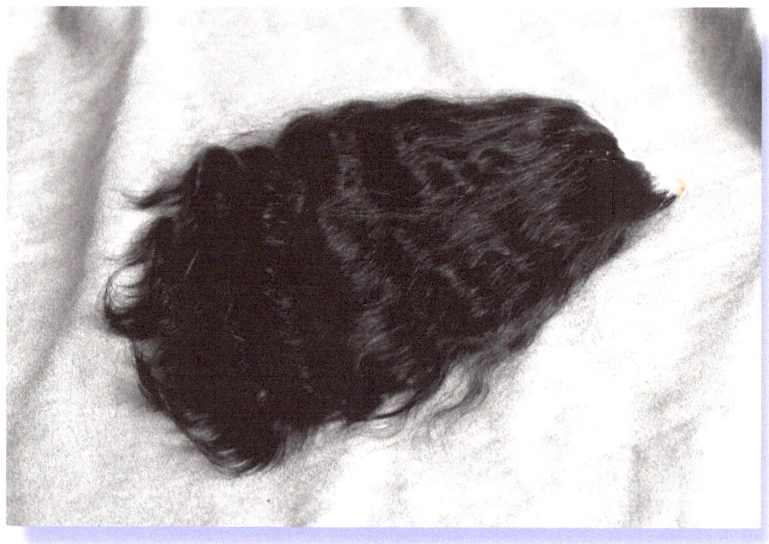

Chapter 5

Making the Wig Cap

The wig cap is the base of the wig—the hat that goes over the doll's head that the hair is attached to. I recommend two different types of wig cap for the two different wig techniques. I think one of them is at a higher difficulty level to create, as it requires a little more meticulousness than the other. Either way, making a wig cap is generally easy and cheap, so if you mess one up, it's no big deal to throw it out and start a new one.

The Solid Wig Cap

The **Solid Wig Cap** is recommended for the **Gluing Technique** for attaching hair and what I consider to be the more relaxed way to make a wig cap. It is a solid "cup" molded over your doll's head using a stretchy fabric with your choice of glue.

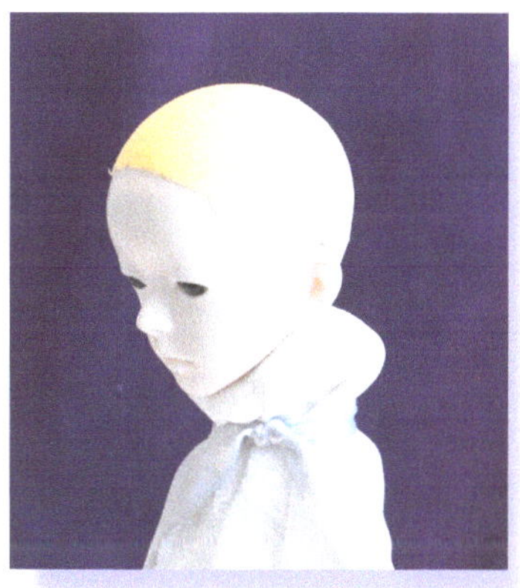

<u>You will need:</u> The doll, the glue of your choice, the fabric of your choice (we'll talk about these choices below), tidy supplies like paper towels and a table covering, paintbrush, cup of water, scissors, stretchy hair ties as well as thin rubber bands, and a pencil.

Fabric

There are a number of different fabrics to choose from, but the best may be a stretchy knit. You can find this at your local craft/fabric store. If you are in the habit of looking closely at fabrics, you will find they all have a grain that runs the entire length of the cloth. When you pull with the direction of the grain it does not stretch, if you pull against the grain it will stretch. Try to pick the one that stretches in EVERY direction. If you can't find this, it's ok, just do the best you can. A cheap alternative is to scrap an old t-shirt or spandex garment. Try to find a fabric that is close to the doll's color, this way it may look like a scalp if it shows between the parted hair. It does not have to be a perfect match.

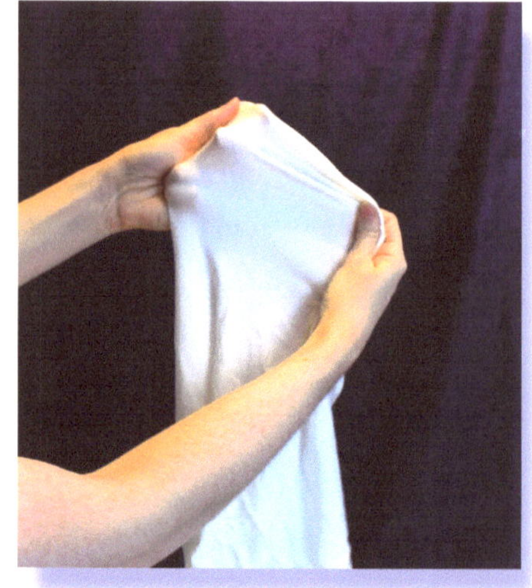

My Two Cents: A lot of artists on the internet prefer pantyhose, but I do not. I feel it is too thin and flimsy, though it can be made to work if you really want it to. I'll just stick with the knit.

Glue

The main choices are PVA (white) glue, like Mod Podge, and then there's liquid latex. My favorite of all is the latex. This is the same stuff marketed for makeup effects. You should be able to find it anywhere special effects makeup is sold, or online. Unless you have a lot of uses for it already, then you can get away with buying the smallest bottle (usually 4 0z). The latex dries fast and holds the hair permanently and expertly. It fixes to the hair instantly, no holding in place and waiting for it to dry! The only downside is that some people are allergic to latex, so please take care—latex made for makeup will be easier on human skin. Regardless of which kind of glue you are using, I will refer to it as "glue" for the rest of this book.

Note: If you are using latex you will NOT need a cup of water because the latex will not wash out of the brush. You will need a cup of water if you are using white glue.

Warning: Liquid latex is easily removed from plastic and skin, but NOT fibers. Therefore please make sure your doll is naked for this process to protect their expensive clothes. The latex will also not wash out of your paint brush, so make sure you are ok with it becoming a permanent rubber tool. No need to discard the brush afterward, hang onto it as it may come in handy for future projects. One more warning, keep the latex away from your own hair as well as the parts of the doll's hair where you do not want it showing!

Ready to get started? Go ahead and set up your work space, cover the table in whatever will protect it from drippy glue, and spread your tools so that they are easy to reach. If you have a cup of water, put it furthest away so you don't accidentally knock it over.

Note: If you have a doll with rooted hair, you may have to remove the hair or cut it off in order to make/use this wig.

Place your doll on the table and cover his/her body in plastic or an old towel.

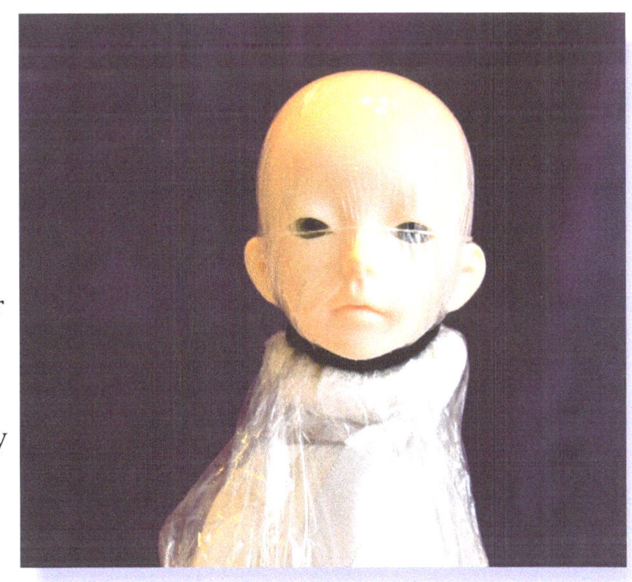

I have a BJD head display stand rigged up so you will be seeing that in the photos. Now cover your doll's head in plastic and as neatly and flatly as you can.

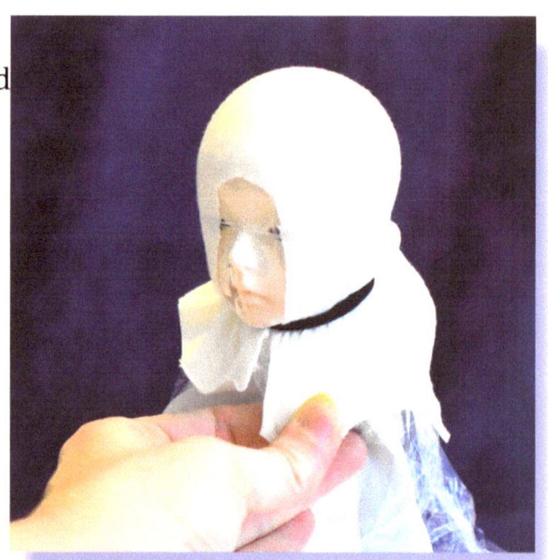

Drape a square of your stretchy fabric over the head and tie it closed around the neck like a lollypop (same if you are using pantyhose), I use an elastic hair tie for this. Pull the fabric in every direction through the tie, stretching the fabric as far as it will go.

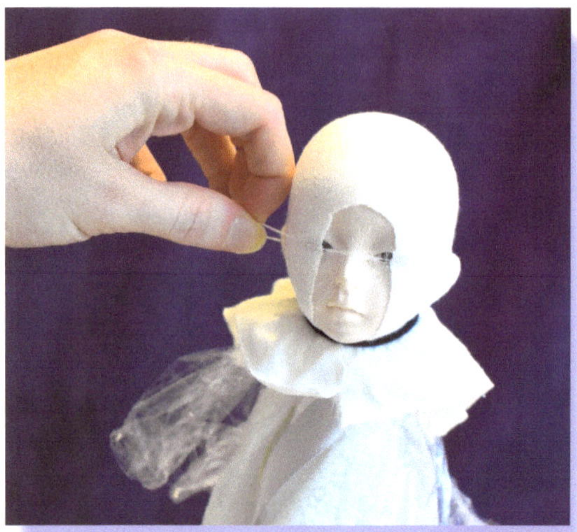

Next grab your thin rubber bands. I have the small, clear plastic type found in the hair accessories section at the grocery store. Place this rubber band over the doll's ears and eyes, sometimes under the nose if it has 3D eyelashes, and around the back as low as possible. This will press the fabric down to the shape of the head, getting a more flush fit.

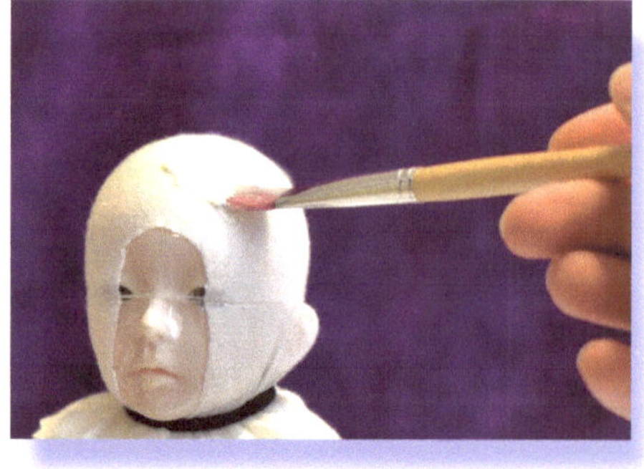

Now the fun part! Grab your glue and your paint brush and start painting glue all over the crown of the head. Make sure to spread it far and wide, even past the area where you think the wig cap will end—even over the doll's forehead. Make the coat even all around. When you have covered the entire area, let dry, and then repeat at least twice.

Note: If you are using PVA glue, remember to rinse your brush after each session, and lay flat to dry. Don't leave the brush standing in the cup of water.

After the final coat is dry, grab a pencil and draw a hairline and part line for the wig. Then carefully remove the rubber bands and lift the cloth and plastic off the doll's head. The plastic will probably be stuck to the fabric so just tear it off carefully.

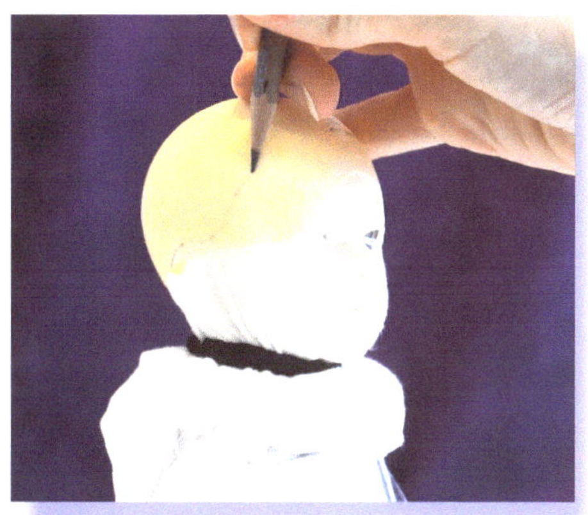

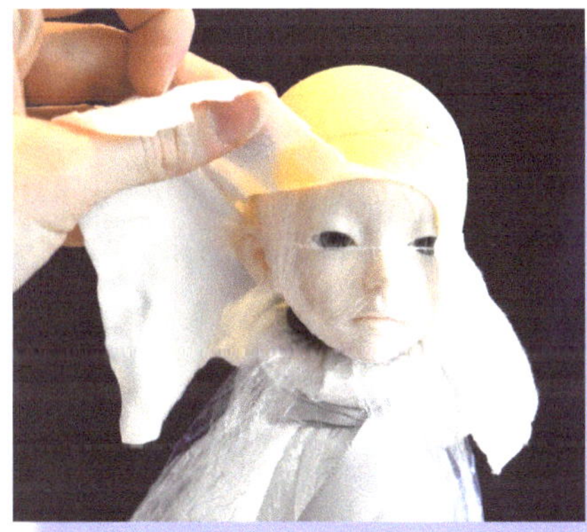

With the plastic and rubber bands removed, use your scissors to cut out the hair line. It's very important that you cut on the OUTSIDE of the pencil line. Cut out MORE than the designated wig cap area, just in case. You can always trim excess later, or you might wind up keeping it. Now you have a wig cap! Place it on your doll's head and relish in the snug custom fit.

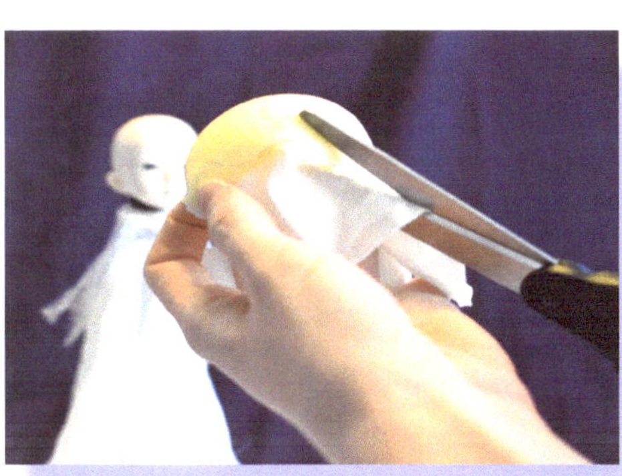

The Tulle Wig Cap

The **Tulle Wig Cap** is made of a fine net (most commonly used in ballet tutus and formal gowns). It is recommended for the **Rooted** wig technique because it has many holes covered in a thin membrane of glue, making it easy to pass a needle through hundreds of times. We will be gluing strips of tulle in a grid pattern over the doll's head for a custom fit. I think of it like papier-mâché. This method may be a little more complex and require meticulous attention. You may have to make two or more before you are satisfied with the quality, but as long as persistence is applied, anyone can do this method.

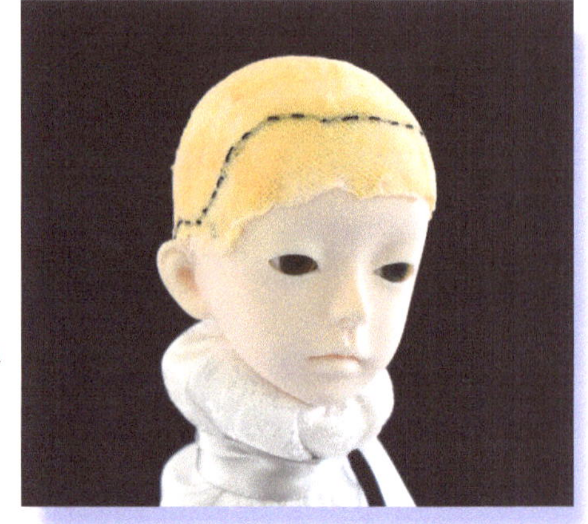

<u>**You will need:**</u> Tulle (one yard is plenty, try to get a color similar to your doll), scissors, glue of your choice, plastic wrap, thin rubber bands, cup of water (if you are using PVA glue), paint brush, table covering, paper towels, sewing needle, sewing thread similar to either the hair color or the tulle color.

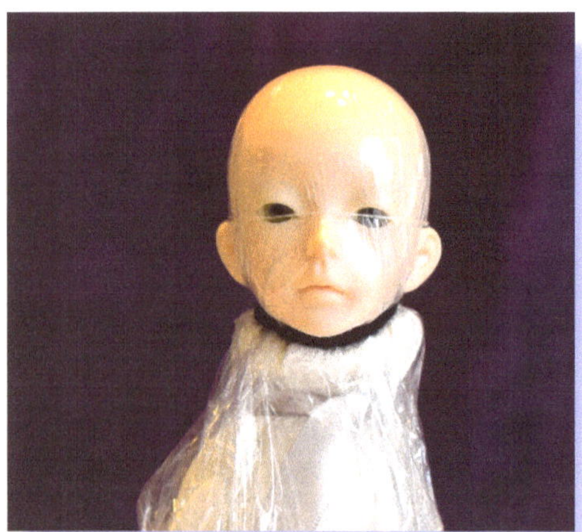

Set up your table as always, cover your doll up to protect them from glue, and put plastic wrap over the head, securing it with a band around their neck (like a lollypop). Now stretch a thin rubber band around the head, over the eyes (or under the nose if they have 3D eyelashes), atop the ears, and around the back of the head as low as possible. This secures the plastic down flush over the head's shape.

Next, cut out a few rectangular strips of tulle. Don't bother measuring the strips in uniform rectangles, just eyeball it and make them different lengths. Cut out at least ten, keeping in mind that you can cut more as needed, but I usually wind up cutting existing strips down instead of gathering more from the tulle bulk.

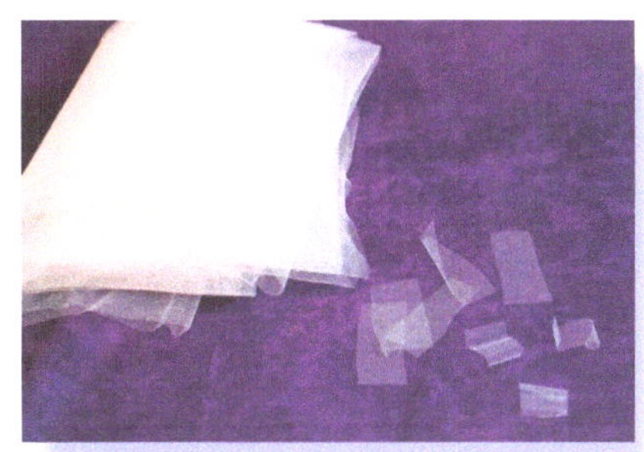

Now open up your glue bottle and/or pour it into a disposable pan, have your paintbrush, paper towel, and water cup handy. Pick up your longest tulle rectangle and place it on the doll's head running front to back; hopefully it will be nice and long and reach all the way from the doll's forehead or eyes to the back of their neck. If it doesn't reach all the way you can apply another strip to fill the gap. Place it and then paint it down onto the plastic wrap with your glue and brush.

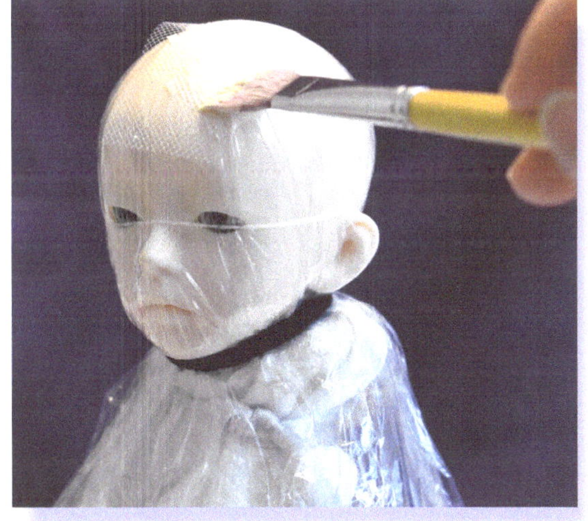

Have your scissors ready also. If your rectangle is particularly wide then you will see tulle sides sticking up and arching. Fixing arches is easy and will be part of the process of "sculpting" this wig

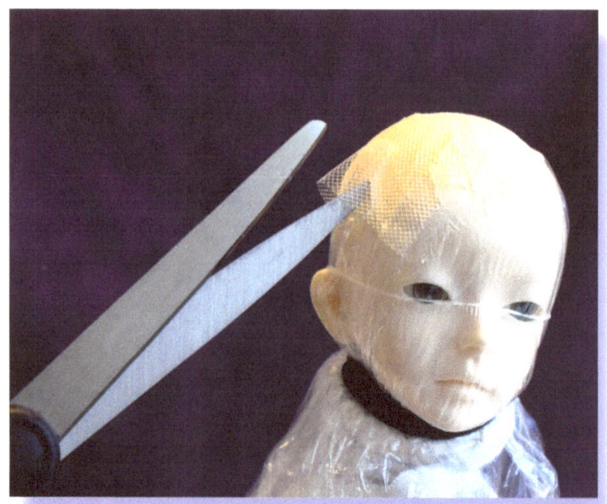

cap. Just clip a slit in the arches. Now you'll have two flaps which can be laid down and overlapped, so lay/overlap them and paint them down. They should stay down without a fight.

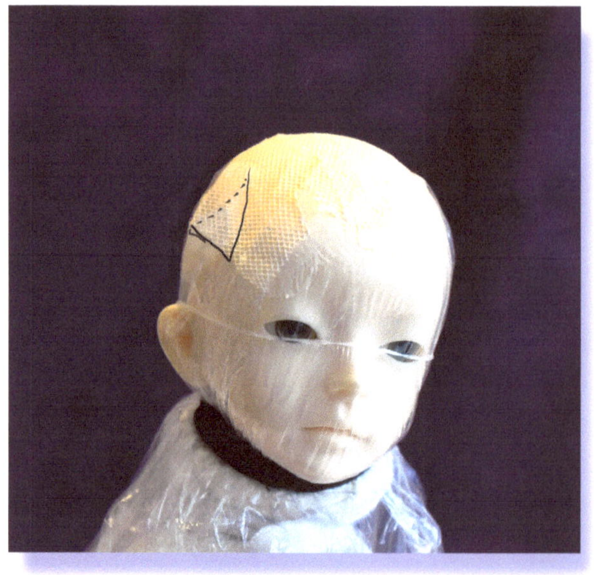

Next, grab another tulle rectangle and place it alongside the first rectangle and paint it down. Clip corners. Make this second rectangle overlap the first one slightly. Continue these steps until the whole crown is covered with one layer of tulle. Take care around the ears/sideburns, and back of the head, making sure these areas get the same thickness as the rest of the wig cap.

Now we will do one more layer of tulle running across the sides of the head to complete the grid pattern. This layer will overlap all previous layers and create a strong united structure. So go ahead and layer them on, clip corners, and take care around the ears and base of the skull. Afterward you can quality check the layers. If you see thin parts, just cut a little square patch of tulle and paint it over the thin area. I usually have to do this around the ears.

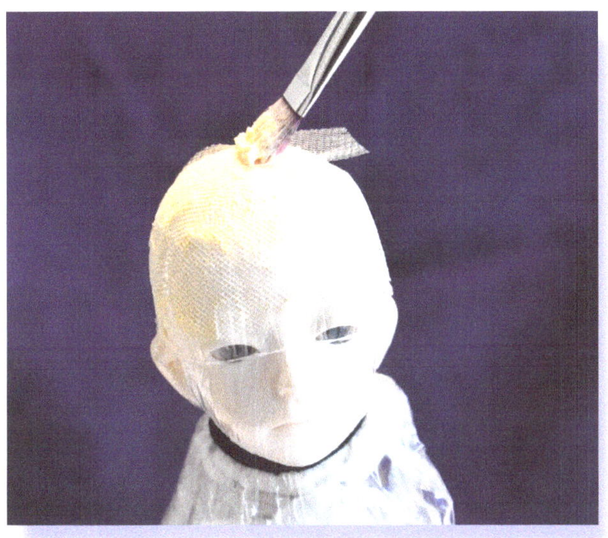

Now let it dry overnight.

When the wig cap is all dry, use a pencil to draw the hairline and the part line before carefully remove the rubber bands and lift the whole thing off the doll head. Peel the plastic wrap from the inside.

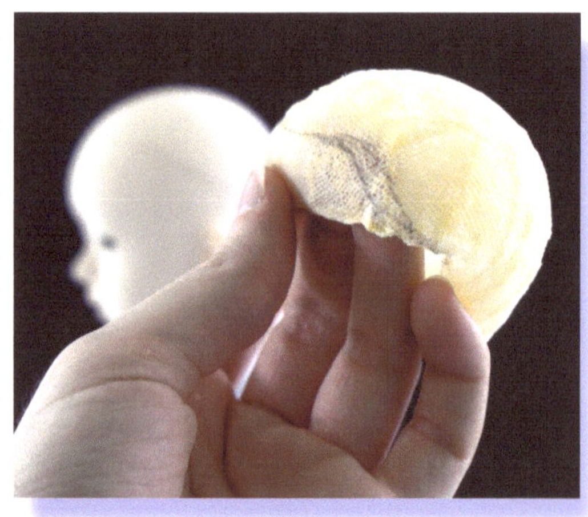

For the next part I have grown to prefer not to cut the hairline until the wig is near complete, especially at the forehead area because I use it as a handhold for sewing.

Next you will need a needle and thread. If you are not keen on sewing, don't worry, just follow these steps of how to do a "backstitch" and you will be fine. Thread your needle and make the ends even for a doubled thread.

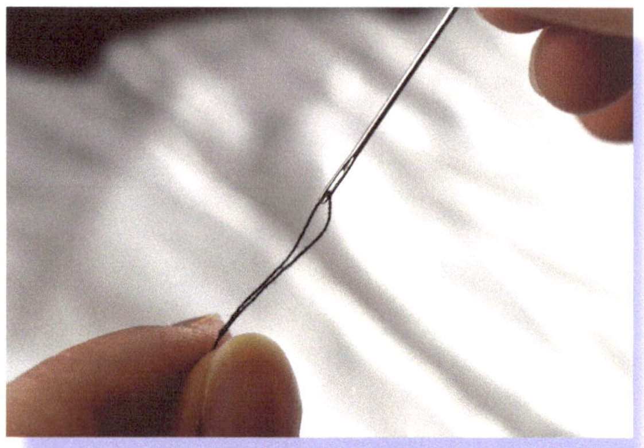

Now tie a knot in the end. One trick for doing this is to wrap the thread around your index finger once or twice and then twist the loop off your finger, grab the end, and pull until the loop settles into a knot.

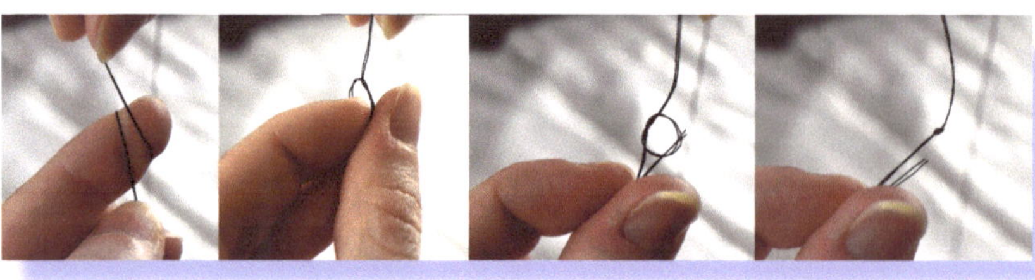

Now you are ready to sew. Here's how to do a backstitch:

Find a place on the pencil line at the back of the wig cap and stick the needle through from the inside.

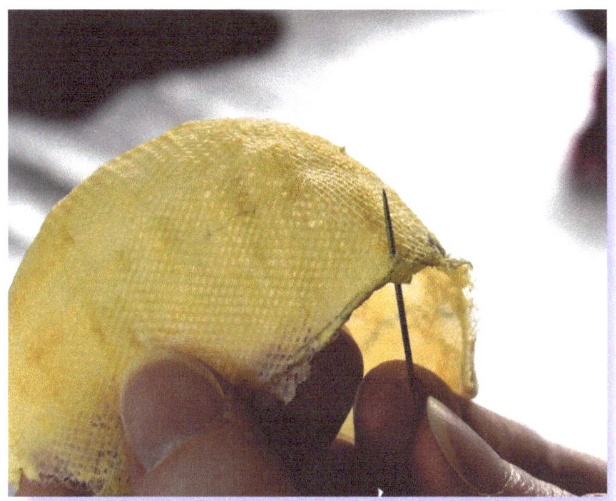

Next stick the needle back into the wig cap, following the pencil line, about 2 or 3 millimeters away from where the needle came out. Any direction is fine. Now you have a little stitch.

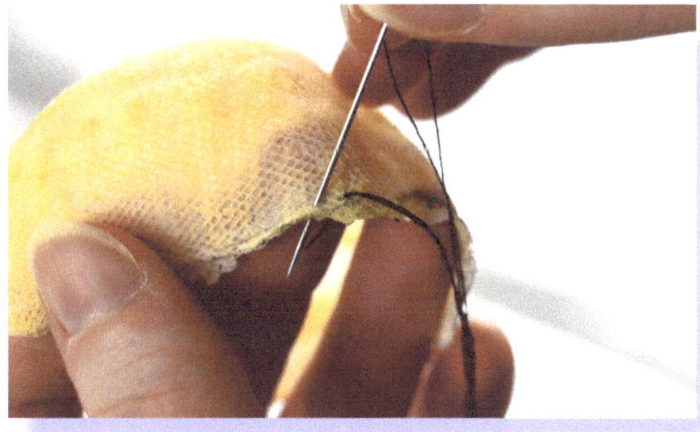

From the underside, push the needle back out, moving the opposite direction. This stitch can be a bit longer, possibly double the length of the one you made on the outside. I call this process "one small step back, one long step forward." The long stitch on the underside should be taking you forward along your path and the smaller stitch on the outside is one small step backward. As you go along making small backstitches, try to use the needle to split the doubled threads on the underside, this will make a nice neat line travelling all around the wig cap.

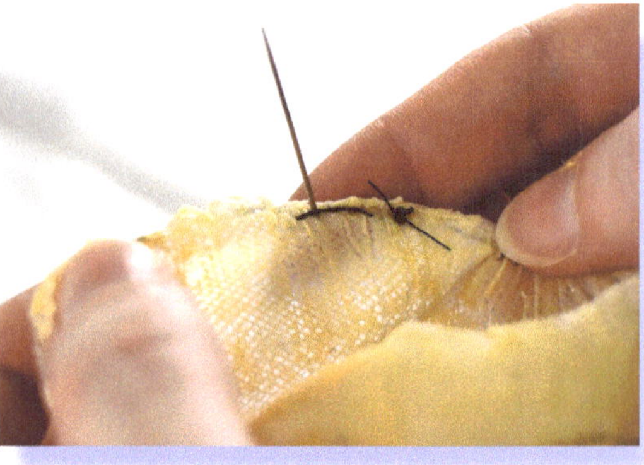

Go ahead and use the backstitch to trace the entire penciled hairline. This new stitched line will make the structure stronger. When you are finished, take your needle to the underside and catch the thread that had been previously applied, send the needle under the thread and notice the loop that forms, put your needle through that loop and pull until it tightens down into a knot, then repeat for a strong doubled knot. And then cut the thread.

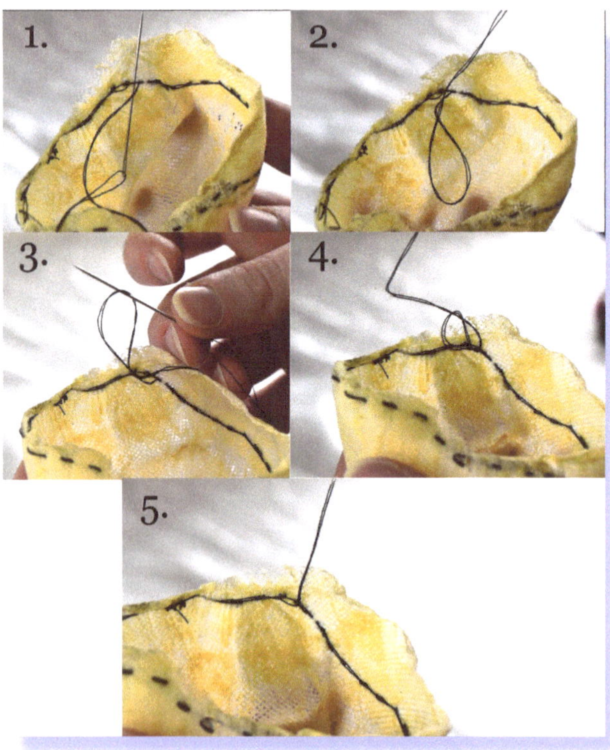

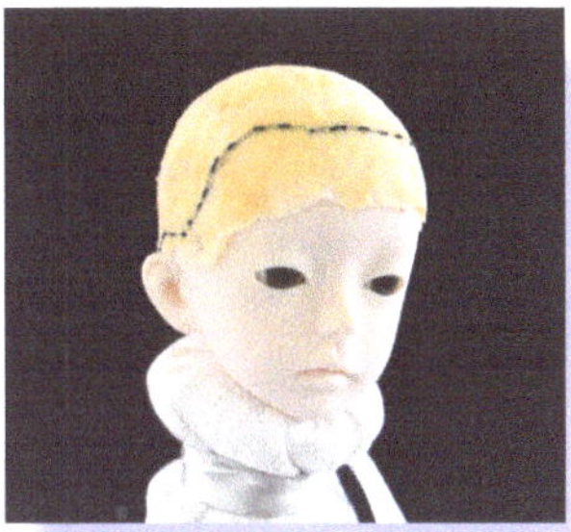

Now you can place the wig cap on the doll's head and bask in the sight of your custom made wig cap. In the next few sections we will attach hair.

Design Choices

Now you've learned how to make two different types of wig caps. It's time to talk about the process. There is no actual limit to how you can make a wig, just ideas you find good and ideas you find bad. And I only have so many ideas, so if a whim hits you then please don't hesitate to test it out! Professional artists choose and discover their creative plans rather than always rely on someone else telling them how to do it.

Let's say you made the **Tulle Wig Cap** and just decided you would rather glue the hair on than root. No problem. I think this type of wig cap can be glued. But the **Solid Wig Cap** we made with knit fabric may not be so easy to sew delicate hairs through. Depending on the fabric type and glue you chose, it may be too thick. Also the **Tulle Wig Cap**'s holes are perfect guides for choosing where to send the needle in and out, keeping you disciplined; the **Solid Wig Cap** would require a lot of guessing.

However! Some retail doll wigs, you may notice, have a special mesh and silicone patch at the top/front, so that the hair is threaded through for the appearance of a natural scalp showing at the part. Yes, we can pull this off at home! And I will show you how in Chapter 8.

There is one more note I want to make on hairline shape. If you are going for hairline realism, then I recommend drawing that out on the **Tulle Wig Cap**. In this shape you can represent a receding hairline, sideburns, etc., and this is most important if your wig will have a brushed back style. The **Solid Wig Cap** is usually drawn like a cup circling around the crown and its shape is covered by the draping hair. But if the hair is sewn or **Punched** into the wig cap at the front hairline then the hair can be brushed back for a realistic "growing" appearance.

Chapter 6

Attaching Hair

The Gluing Process

For this process you can either use the **Solid Wig Cap** or the **Tulle Wig Cap**.

You will need: Doll head, wig cap, glue, brush, water (for white glue), scissors, plastic wrap, hair, and table and doll coverings.

By now you know the drill—set up the workspace so you don't make a mess, cover the doll so they don't get glue on them or their clothes. Place a piece of plastic wrap over the doll's head to keep the glue off.

Now place your newly-made wig cap over the plastic and in the proper wearing position. It's time to attach hair! So grab a small lock of hair, spread it neatly between your fingers, and trim the top (the end that will be glued) so that it has a straight and even edge.

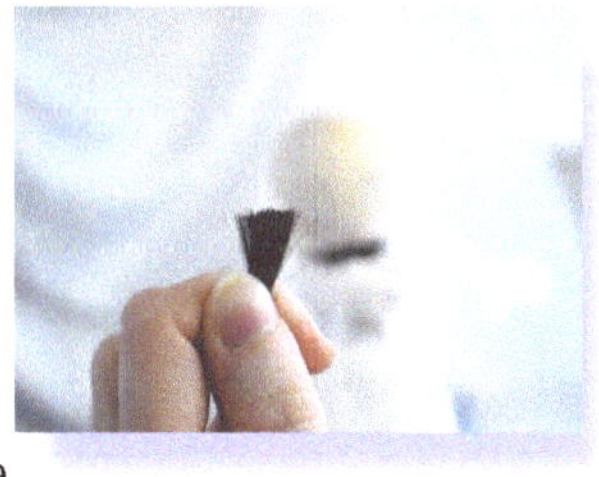

Use your brush to spread a little glue at the bottom center of the wig cap. Remember to place your longest lock here if you are concerned with getting the most out of limited length. With the hair spread and flattened as neatly as you can, place the top of the hair onto the wet glue surface and hold it as you brush more glue over the hair in short upward strokes.

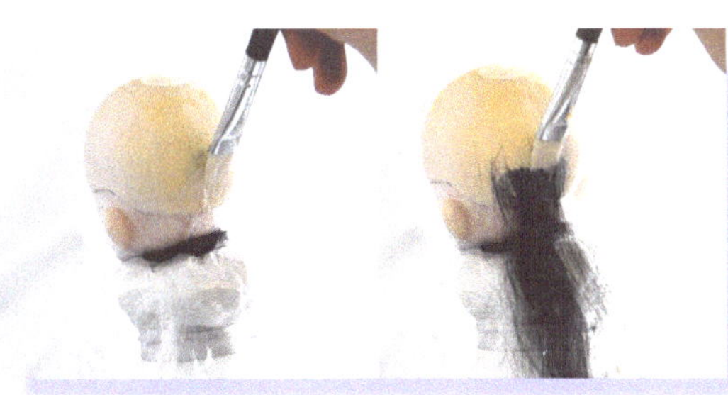

Try to spread the glue evenly and smooth out

the texture. Now you can move to the side and place another lock.

You can glue down an entire horizontal row before having to stop to wait for the glue to dry.

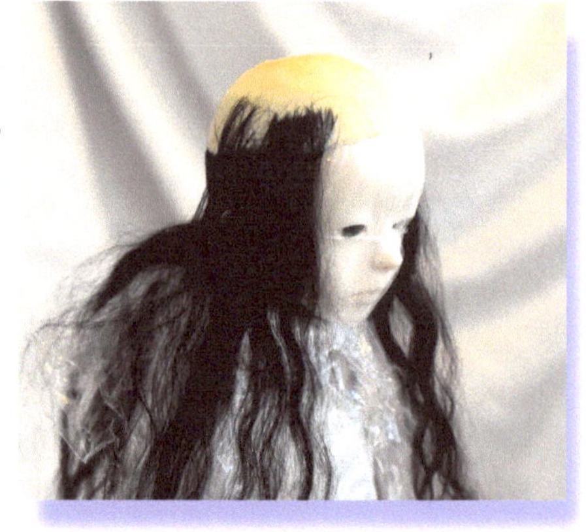

When it dries, move up to the next row. At the back of the wig, you can spread the hair in wide locks and leave a little space between each horizontal tier. Try not to make them too thick or close together. If a bad gap happens or you feel the layer is too thin, just grab some more hair to fill in the gaps and build up the layers. When you get to the sides and top of the hair, your locks may get smaller, more precise, and closer together.

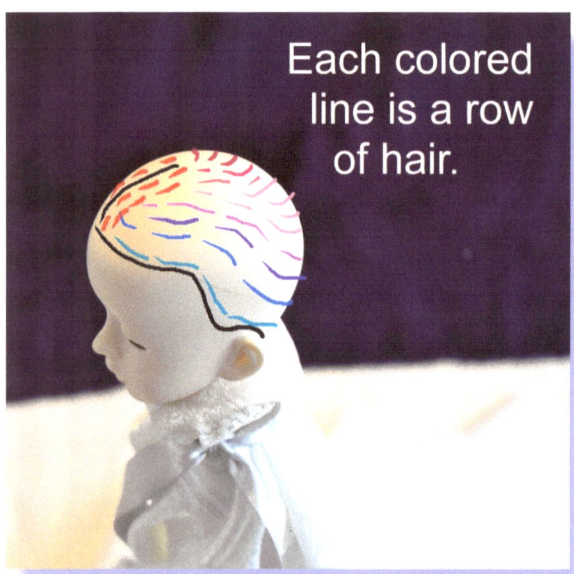

Remember to glue down the hair in directions you want the hair to lay. If you intend to make a high ponytail wig, you can place the glued wefts moving up the back of the head and straight back from the front toward the point where the hair will be gathered together for the ponytail. Don't hesitate to draw a circle on the wig cap where the ponytail will sprout as well as directional arrows if it will help.

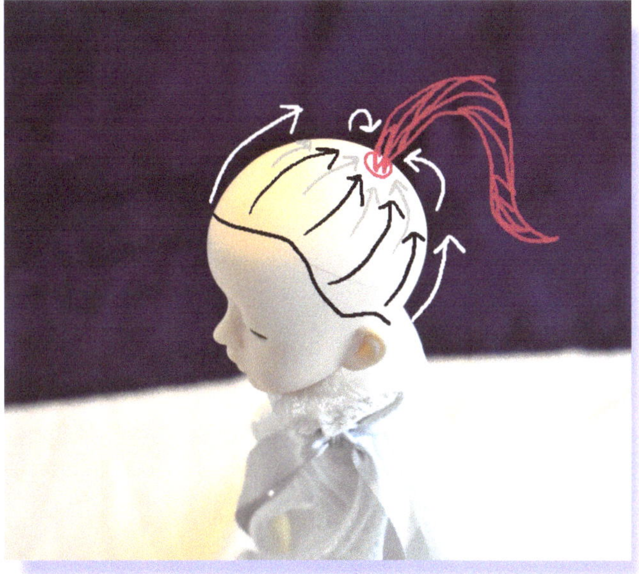

The same rule applies if the wig will be parted on an extreme side of the head, make the hair lay away from the part line.

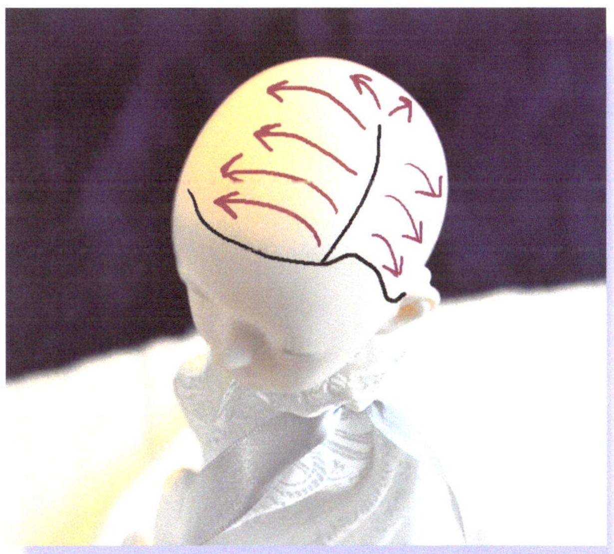

Keep the part line clear of hair and work your way toward it until the glued ends of each opposite side looks at the other. At the end of the process, your part line might be covered in hair but still apparent under the two glued sides.

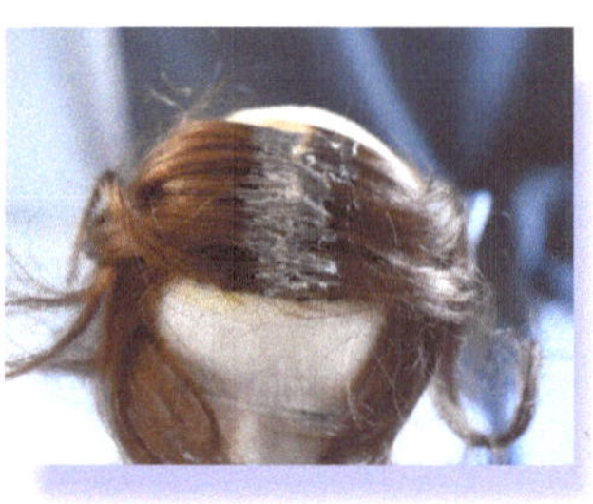

My Two Cents: For a **Glued wig** I really don't like synthetic hair. My favorite hair for this is alpaca or angora mohair. I find synthetic hair to be thick, stiff, stubborn, lumpy, and just downright unpleasant. The alpaca and angora hair is soft and fine and when you paint the glue down over the ends they flatten out beautifully and stick down under the wet glue with little hassle. The synthetic hair tends to clump together and, in its stubborn thickness, is liable to pop up when you most want it to just lie down and wait for the glue to dry. I made my first glued wig with angora mohair and it was a lovely experience with basically no frustration. Even the human hair wig I made did not give me as much trouble. For this book I decided to stage a wig making step using scrap synthetic hair and that is when I noticed that not only was the process annoying, but the resulting workmanship was hideous. Above is a photo of what I came out with. I am not impressed. Below you will see a steep contrast with Angora mohair.

Creating a Part in the Hair

Use your scissors to cut open the wig cap (and glued hair) all the way down the designated pre-drawn part line. It's most likely covered up by glued hair but still obvious.

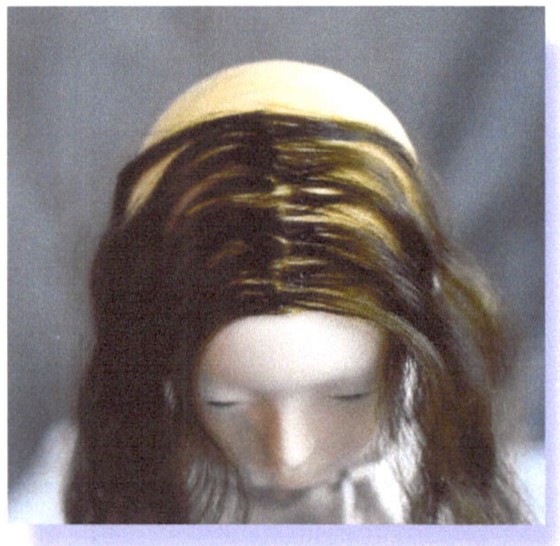

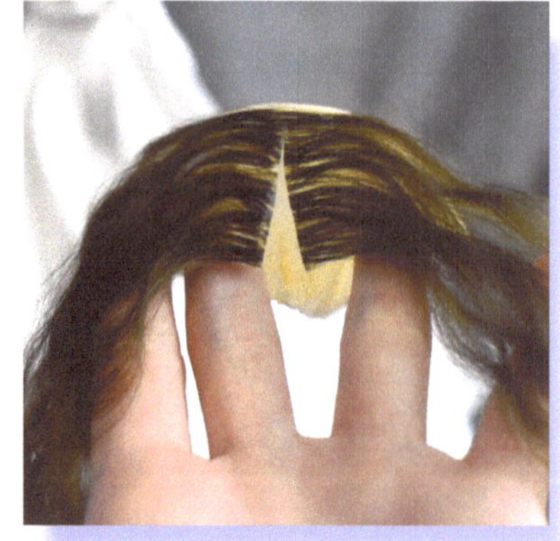

The basic way to make a part line is to glue hair to the INSIDES of the newly cut slit and flip them outside and fold them over like in the photos below. You will need to implement your hot curling iron or straightening iron to make the hair lay down in this fashion.

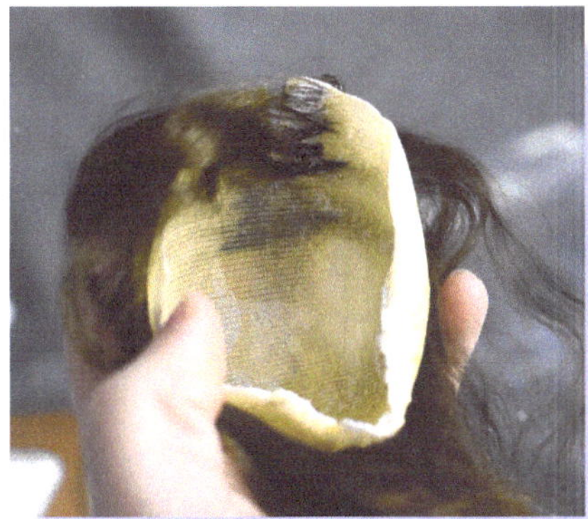

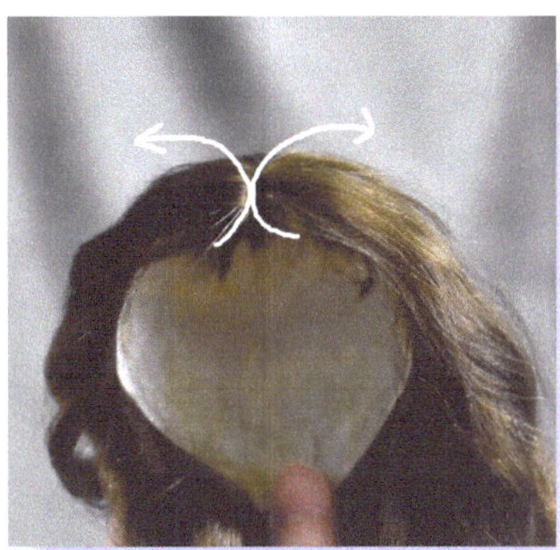

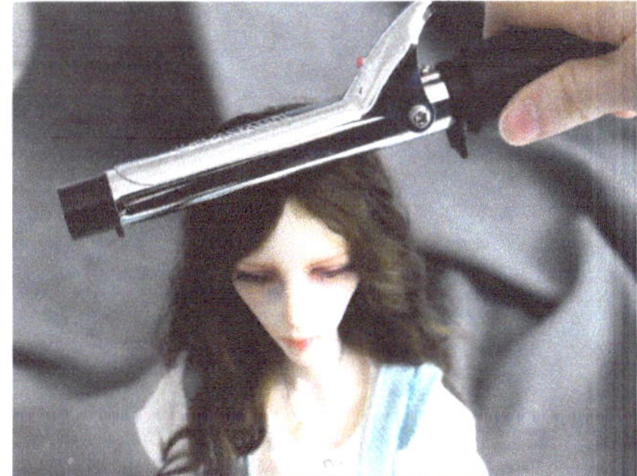

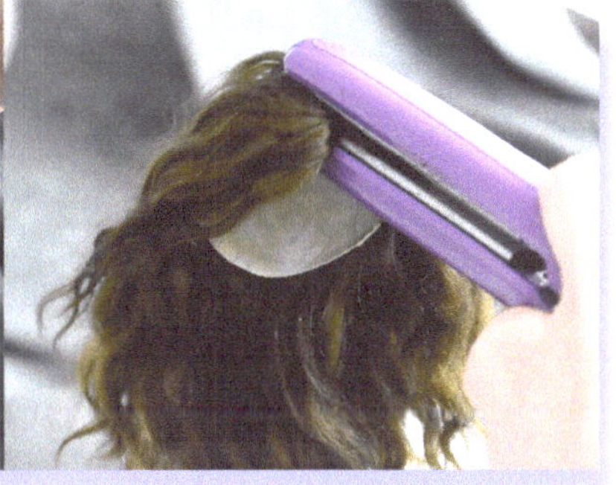

Once you've filled in the entire slit, you will need to cut a square of tulle, fabric, or anything you have on hand to patch the two sides of the slit closed. Just slather some glue down, apply the patch square and then use a clip to hold it all together until the glue dries.

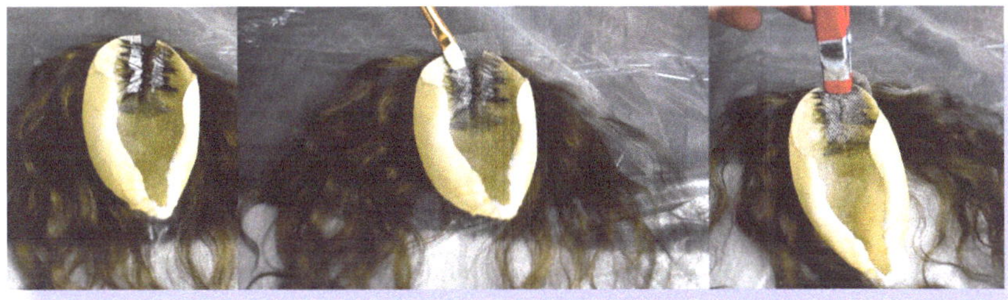

That is just one way to make a part line. I have other methods I will share in Chapter 8, so please read on!

The Rooting Process

This process requires the **Tulle Wig Cap** for a base which will possess holes that are easy to thread the hair through. You won't need the doll's head for this process unless you want it to model the work in progress now and again. This is a versatile wig that can be styled and parted in virtually any way after it is completed.

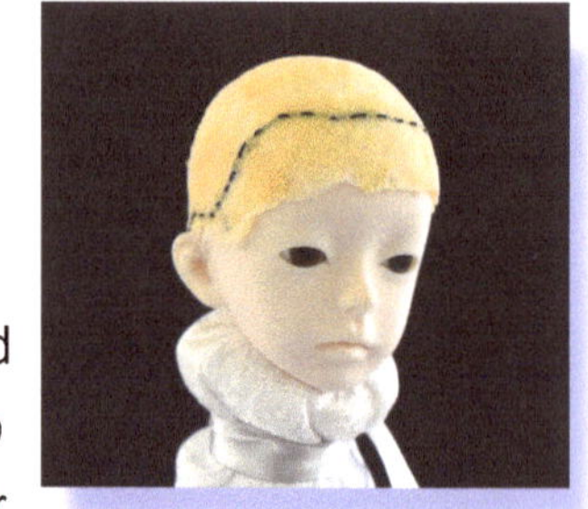

My Two Cents: Human hair is not recommended for rooting. In my experience it was too coarse to work with and the white glue did not hold the hair in for some reason! You could possibly try liquid latex as glue to seal the hair on the inside of the wig cap but beware that liquid latex is thick and may pile up fast, altering the inside fit of the wig cap's size. After several applications, the wig cap may become too small to fit on the dolls' head. But you can try if you are curious enough.

<u>You will need:</u> wig cap, glue, paint brush, beading needle or quick thread needle, comb, hair straightening iron (optional), mineral oil, hair tie, table covering.

The rooting process is a bit different. I am confident that anyone who can't sew can still accomplish this goal. Below I will teach you the basic technique of sewing required. All you need to have is patience, persistence, and discipline. This wig will take a long time and if you don't sit down and do the work, it will never blossom into a completed wig—just become another one of those sad, lonely, discarded projects. Are you ready?

Just like we did in the glued technique, in order to get the most out of a limited length, you'll choose your longest lock and place it at the back center spot of the wig cap.

Needle Options

I recommend a beading needle, the type that is long and thin with a twisted structure so that it has a wide but collapsible eye. If you have trouble threading fine fluffy hair through the eye you can always dip the end in a cup of water to make it stiff and pointy for easier threading.

Or

You can use a quick-threading needle which looks like any basic needle but has an open eye so that you can thread it easily and quickly without any precision skills. Mine looks like this:

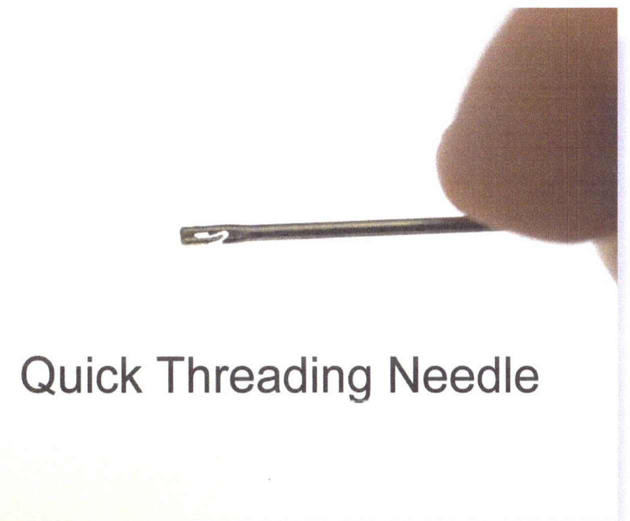

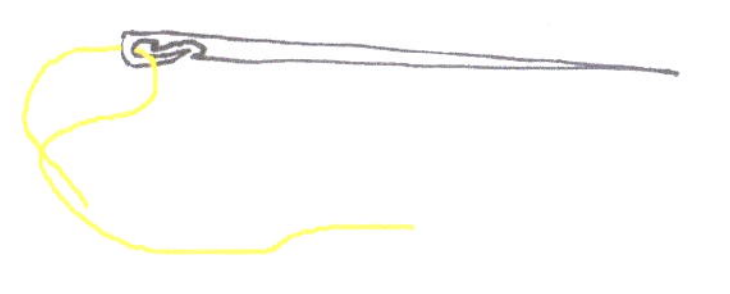

The quick-threading needle allows you to thread by pulling the hair strands taut and grazing it along the side of the needle opening until it catches. The needle I use is one of those as-seen-on-TV items called "The One Second Needle." I got mine on Ebay.

Sewing Technique for the Rooted Wig Process

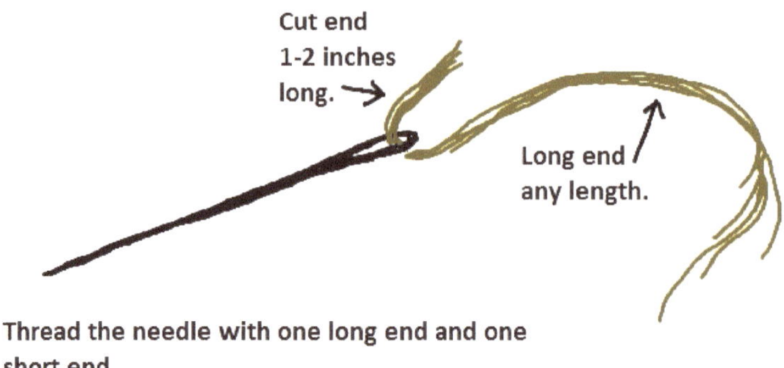

Thread the needle at the cut end of the animal hair which will be cropped evenly, the other end will be tapered as the different lengths of hair within the lock come to an end. Send the needle into the wig cap from the OUTSIDE and then back out. When coming back out, choose a hole in the tulle that is 1 or 2 holes next door to the entrance hole. Don't make the two protruding strands even, one must be long and the other must be short, averaging about 1-2

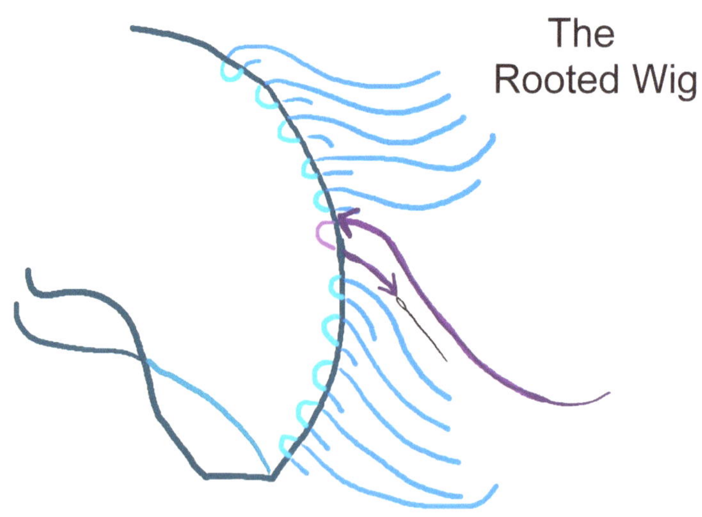

inches long. The cropped end of the hair will be through the exit hole. Ideally, the short exit end should be positioned BELOW the long entrance end. Thus the long end will cover the short end and the wig will look more natural and full.

Be gentle with the wig cap as you work as it's usually easy to warp its shape with aggressive handling. You may find it a challenge to maneuver the needle in and out while also looking at what you're doing, but with practice you will get used to this awkward procedure. In the worst case scenario, the **Tulle Wig Cap** may become warped or damaged and you may resort to starting again with a new wig cap. But fear not because practice makes perfect, wig caps are easy and cheap to remake, you can repair tears with a patch of tulle and glue, and in the event of starting over you can salvage the hair by pulling it out and trying again or by snipping off and reusing hair that has already been glued in.

After you have a few strands sewn in as a group, you'll need to dip your paintbrush into your glue (white glue is recommended unless you find your liquid latex brand to be thin enough not to add bulk) and then brush it gently over the hair on the INSIDE of the wig cap.

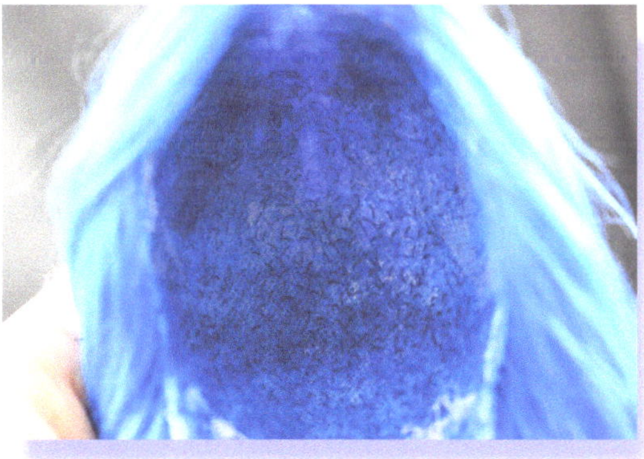

At right: How many strands did I root into this wig? A LOT! But to tell the truth, you can get away with making the roots farther apart around the back and sides of the wig. Make the center-top and front (or where ever you will part the hair) closer together and more numerous as this hair will lay over the rest. If you think there are areas too sparse, you can always add more hair later.

Repeat this process at least a thousand times to fill in the entire wig cap. You may feel discouraged at how pathetic the hair looks after the first few strands are sewn in, but don't lose heart, keep at it, and it will fill in well and look great!

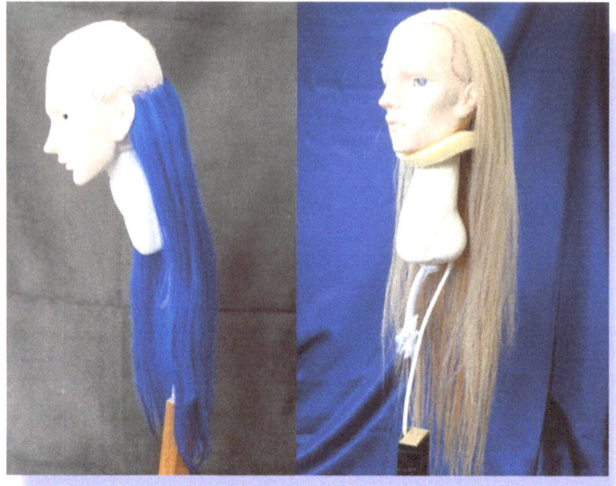

At left: I root my wigs back-to-front.

As you move up the back of the wig cap you may switch to the shorter lengths. There is no science to this, just use your own judgement. How high up do you want to see the next length category? Do you want a layered look at all? Maybe you can use the longest locks for the whole wig for one solitary length. Is the doll's hair short on the sides? Or just in the front? Feel free to use a pencil to mark off sections where other lengths should appear to help you stick to your plan. Also don't forget the drawing you made in the beginning, it should serve as your blueprint.

Note: Sometimes thinly **Rooted** hair can be stylish! My doll Paju's character is an old raggedy vagabond type. His **Tulle Wig Cap** matches his pink resin color well. So after my first wave of rooting, I noticed it was a little thin around the top where it should have been thicker. Normally I would have taken my needle and hair out again to sew in more where needed, but I liked it that way so I left it as is.

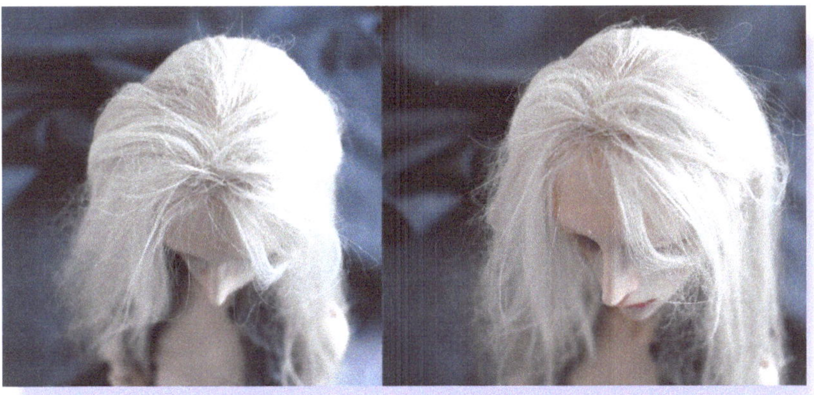

Above: You can see the peachy color of Paju's head glowing through the thinness of the hair. I could have sewn in more hair, but I liked this style as is.

Take Care of the Hair as You Root

You will be working on your **Rooted** wig for a long time, perhaps weeks. And since it requires a certain amount of manhandling you'll want to be conscientious of the hair already sewn in. If you follow a few steps you will not only protect the hair but also transform it into beautiful.

Once the hair sewn in is at a certain thickness (I'll let you be the judge of that), you'll want to comb it. Put a little oil on your comb—just a tiny bit on the first combing—and then comb the hair. Some hair may fall out and that's ok, just be gentle. The hair falling out may possibly be a good thing, unless of course the comb is pulling out entire locks sewn in, in this case you may need to reinforce the glue on the inside of the wig cap.

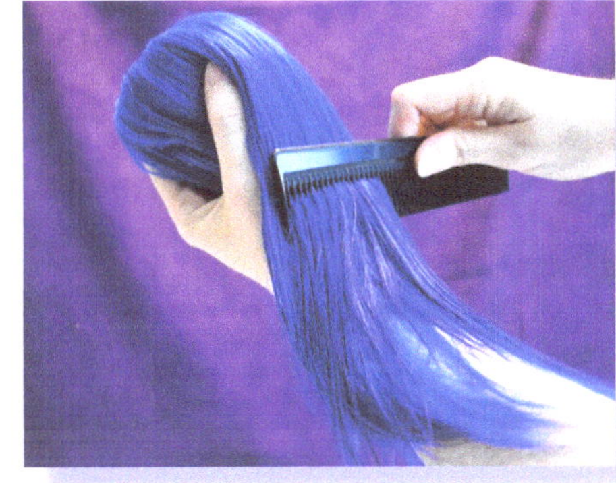

When the hair is thick enough to hold then you can proceed to put a hair tie around it. This will keep the hair wrangled and neat as you continue to work. Use a good ponytail band or scrunchy, do NOT use a common rubber band!

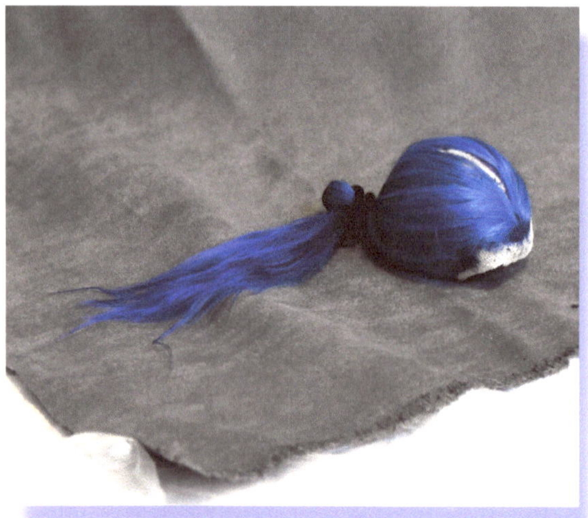

When the hair is ponytailed you will easily be able to see how much work you've done since combing. As you continue and notice that there is a lot of new messy hair hanging out, you can release the ponytail, oil up your comb, and comb the new hair into the old.

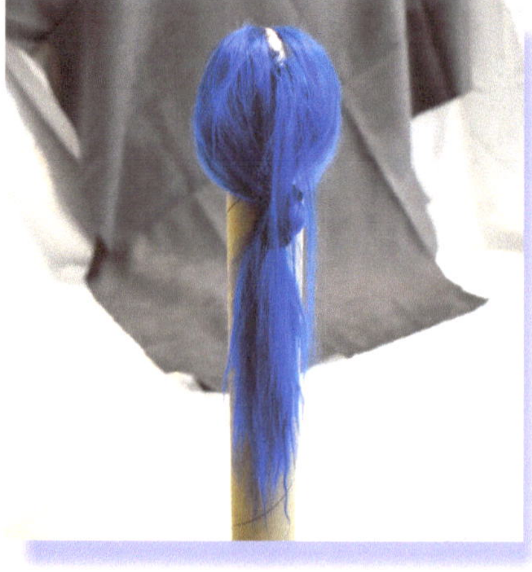

You'll notice that each combing improves the quality of the hair more and more. But try not to oil the comb too much because too much oil with make the hair look wet. You can usually skip re-oiling it a few times. If you do happen to over oil then the only way to fix it is to wash the hair with soap again. But don't worry, each type of wig cap can handle this. Just be sure to let the wig and wig cap dry completely before continuing work.

Chapter 7

Bonus Technique: The Punched Wig

I have another wig option for you! Once again, this option is completely tailored to your doll's unique head shape. The **Punched** wig is designed to look like it has a natural scalp with hair growing right out of it. This is usually called "hair punching" as it's very similar to how the filmmakers create realistic human head props.

My Two Cents: I just want to give you a bit of warning about this option that I have not perfected it for myself and can't guarantee that it will be a good option for you. The hair punching technique tended to break large holes into my **Tulle Wig Cap**, though such damage can easily be repaired by applying a tulle patch with glue to the inside of the wig cap. Also, punching the hair did not save me any time, in fact it cost more time considering I was already good at using a quick-threading needle to root the hair in, I was a little clumsy with this one. I recommend trying the **Solid Wig Cap** for hair punching. Also, practice on a scrap wig cap if you have one, or make two on purpose just for this reason. Nonetheless, I'm happy to share this idea with you just in case you can make it work!

You will need: Doll head, hair of choice (any kind), sewing needle, a **Tulle** or **Solid Wig Cap**, felting needle (it has barbed sides), Styrofoam ball with the same circumference as the doll's head or slightly smaller, scissors, plastic wrap, rubber bands, liquid latex, acrylic paint (optional), comb, and mineral oil (if you are using natural animal hair).

Making the Wig Cap

You can try using the **Tulle** or **Solid Wig Cap** for this technique, it's your choice. However you MUST use liquid latex for this process. Liquid latex basically comes in two colors, white and flesh colored.

If you have a beige colored doll, then the flesh tone latex should be ok. It would be a great idea to brush some latex onto something and let dry to sample the color. If it matches the doll then great. If not then you can always add acrylic paint to the wet liquid latex to change its color. Yes this does work! You may need to practice with your color mixing and dry-matching to design a formula before starting the final wig cap.

Note: If you need to color your latex with acrylic paint then it is ok to use the cheap craft paint.

Now place the wig cap over a Styrofoam ball (perhaps a life-sized Styrofoam head if your doll is life-sized). You can rig up an easy wig stand using a Styrofoam ball, paper towel roll, and square of cardboard all glued together. I recommend making this as it's a good place for your wig to rest when not being worked on or used. Otherwise you'll need to prop the ball and wig cap on something so you can work. Perhaps sticking it on one of those paper spikes would help.

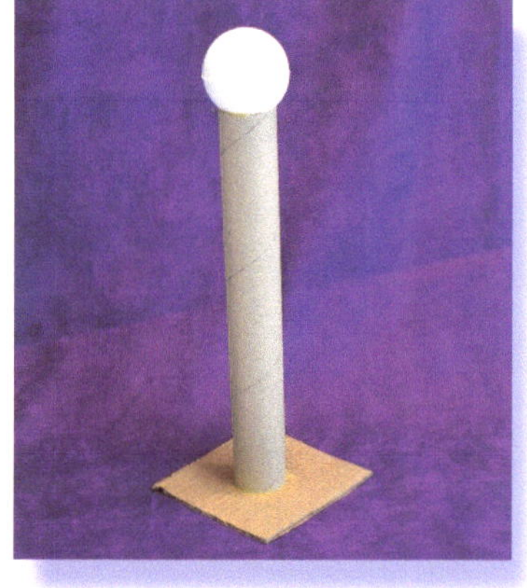

Cheap and easy wig stand made of cardboard or...

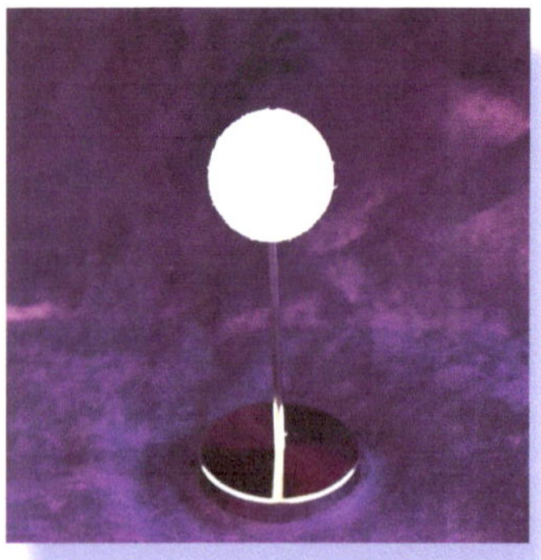

Styrofoam ball stuck on a note spike.

Attaching Hair to the Punched Wig

You have a few options and first I will recommend the quickest, easiest method. We will revisit the **Gluing Technique** for this. Just like in the **Gluing Technique** you will need to start gluing locks to the back/bottom of the wig cap. **<u>Use liquid latex as glue</u>**. Stop gluing about half an inch away from the part and the hairline (perhaps more on a doll larger than 1/3). Next, we will change techniques.

Hair Punching

Ideally, this should create a realistic look of hair growing out of skin, we need to use special tools, the first of which is a regular sewing needle with a modified eye. You will need to use wire cutters to cut open the eye of the needle. Please wear safety glasses while doing this. You can also use an electric grinding tool, like a Dremel, to grind an opening into the eye. As a result your needle eye should be hooked and look like this:

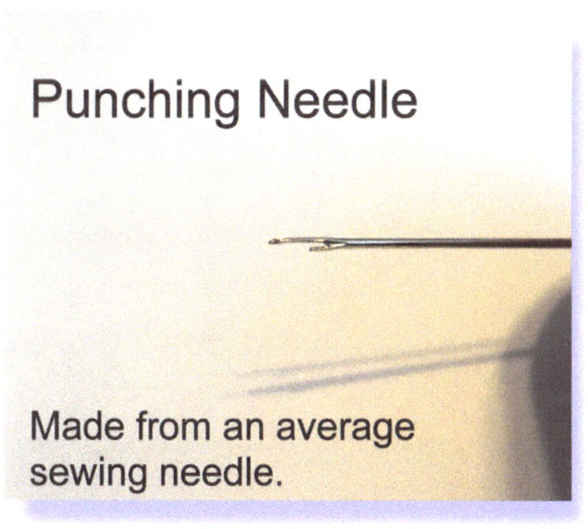

This tool is good for working with thick hair like human or synthetic. You will need to count out and punch only two or three hairs at a time for the most realistic effect. Well, you can do larger groups of hair if you are still somewhat back on the head, but the closer to the front you come, the less hair at a time you need to punch.

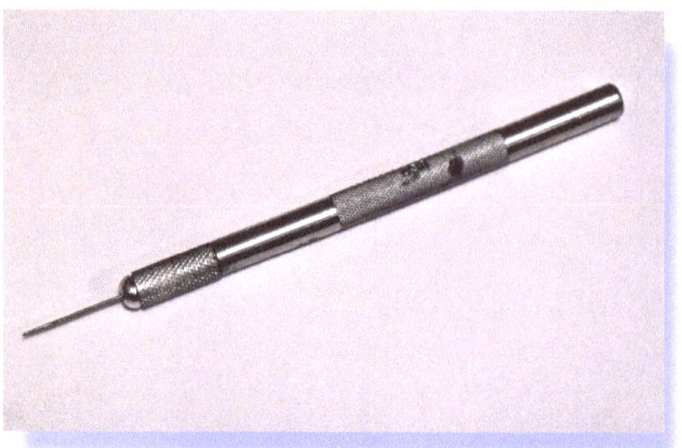

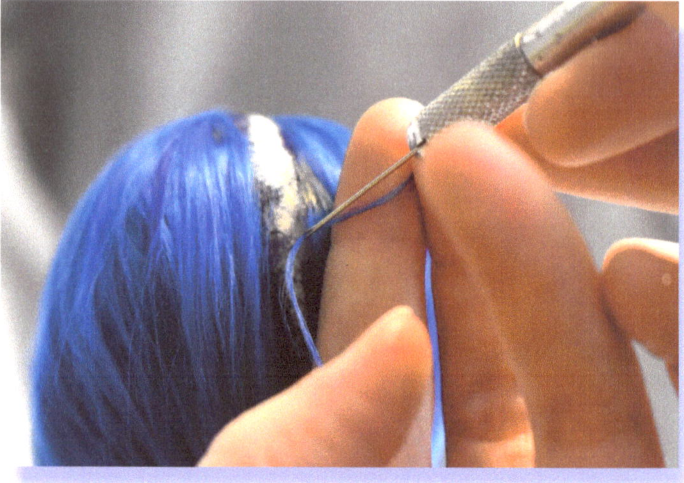

Above: Use the modified sewing needle eye to punch small groups of hair into the wig cap. It is recommended to secure the needle into a craft knife handle.

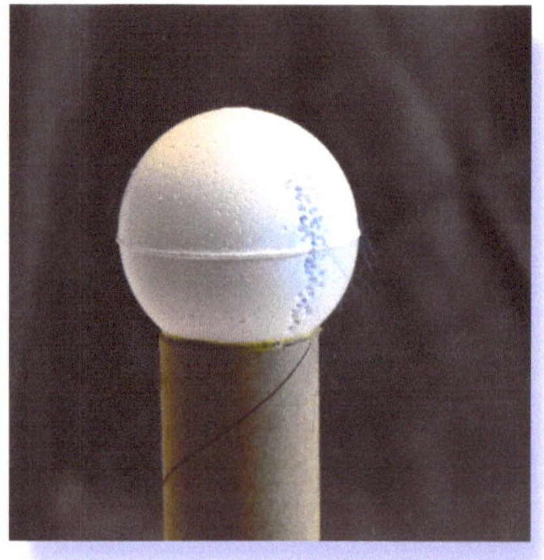

At left: This is my Styrofoam ball after a few rounds of hair punching. Be very careful when removing the wig from the ball because some of the hair may be stuck and come out of the wig upon removal!

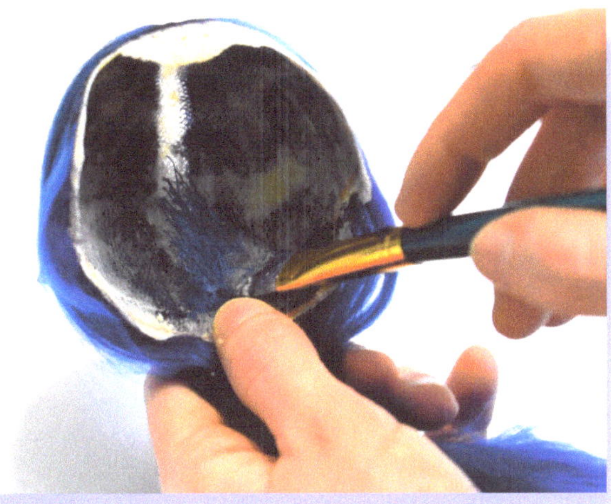

Above: Gluing down the **Punched** hair ends on the inside of the wig cap.

You can finish off the wig this way or...

Hair Felting

You can use a felting needle if you are using extra fine wooly hair, especially wool roving. In fact the felting needle did not work with my alpaca hair so you may want to limit its use to wool roving. The felting process is best for the very front of the hair, you can still use the previous tools and techniques for the backside of the wig and reserve felting for the front. This process is faster than **Rooting** or **Punching**. The **Solid Wig Cap** should work well for this.

The concept of using the felting needle is that it has barbs on its sides which catches small amounts of hair and drags it down through the wig cap's latex surface.

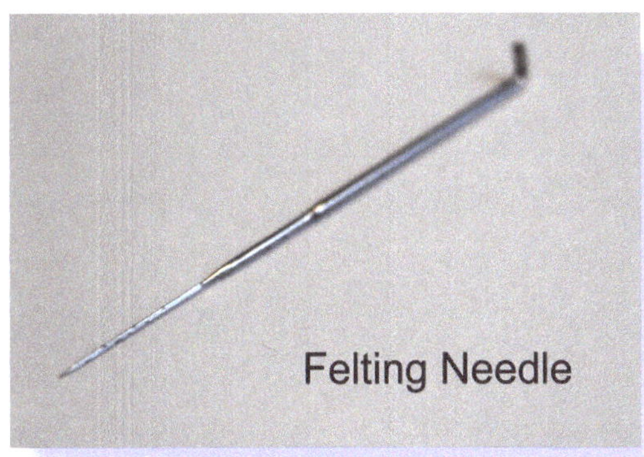

Place the wig cap over a Styrofoam ball because the needle is expected to penetrate through the cap and into the Styrofoam. When the needle exits, it leaves the hair stuck in the rubber wig cap. In theory, the flexible rubber closes over the hair and holds it in place, however it will not hold with 100% strength. In order to seal the hair in tight and allow for future combing sessions you will need to seal the hair from the inside of the wig cap with glue or liquid latex.

Grab a lock of hair, fan it a bit in your fingers and lay it on the wig cap.

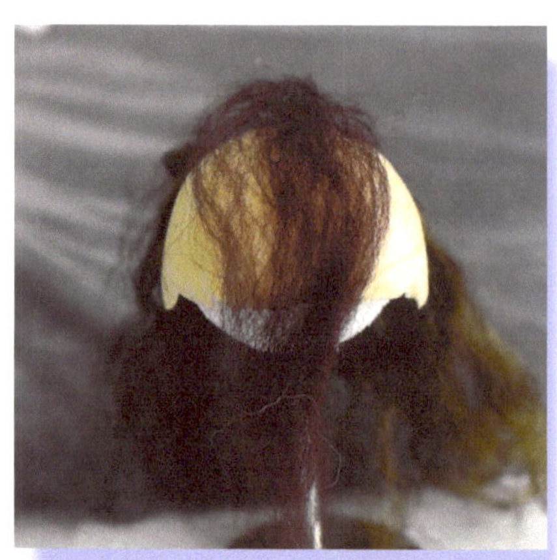

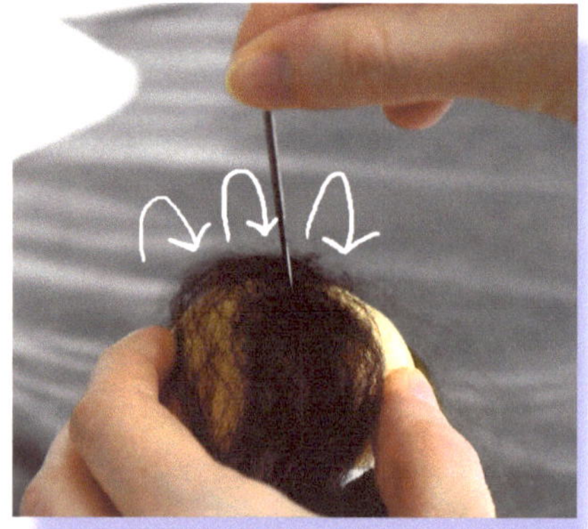

Then rapidly punch the needle through the wig cap and Styrofoam as if your hand were a sewing machine. Do this in rows.

When you are finished, or just have a lot **Punched** in, you can carefully remove the cap from the Styrofoam (the hair might cling to the Styrofoam, so take care) and then dip a small and new paintbrush into the liquid latex and gently brush it onto the inside of the cap, flattening all the hairs down. After it dries, proceed to gently pull the loose hairs away which will leave you with the remaining secured hair. Then repeat the process of punching, gluing, and tugging until the cap is as full as you need it.

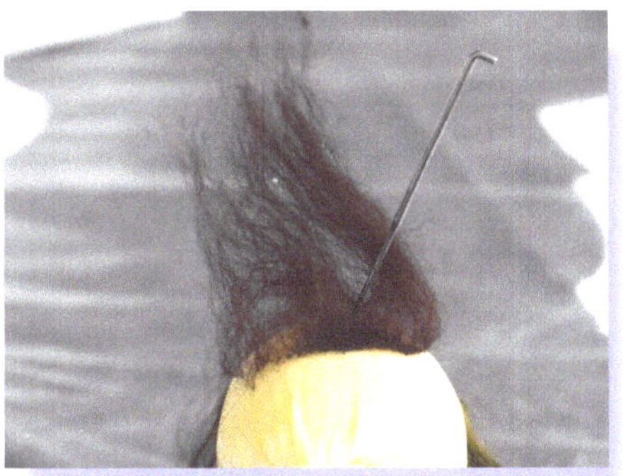

Above: A side of the wool roving stands on end after one row of punching. This is a good way to make mohawks and other crazy shapes!

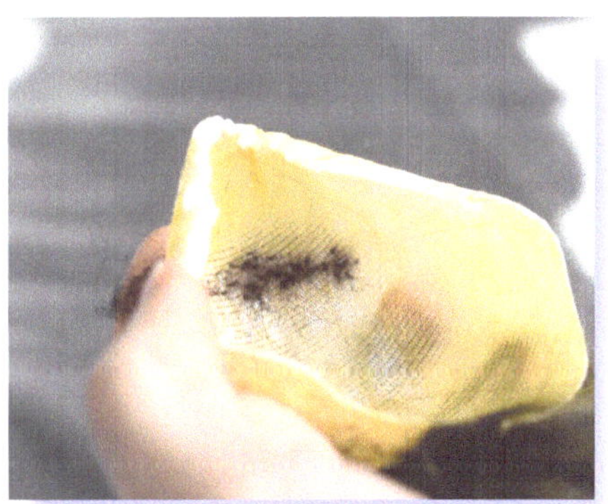

Above: The inside of the wig cap after a row of **Punched** wool roving. Remember to glue down the inside before removing the loose hair on the outside.

Chapter 8

Technique Blending

Now that we've learned three different ways to make wigs, we can stretch our minds to even more possibilities. I'm sure you can think of a few yourself, but for now I will share at least one that I know.

Glued Wig with Rooted Hair Part

You might have seen something similar to this when you bought a wig. Some factory-made wigs wanted to give you a fashionable parted look rather than the spiraled technique of old. They did this by sewing the long hair weft into a U-shape rather than a spiral and then adding a patch of silicone to the front/top of the wig cap and rooting hair into it so that it looks like the hair is growing out of a scalp. We can do this too!

First make a **Solid Wig Cap** just like in Chapter 5 using either glue or liquid latex. After it dries, draw a section for a cut out shape where the hair part would be.

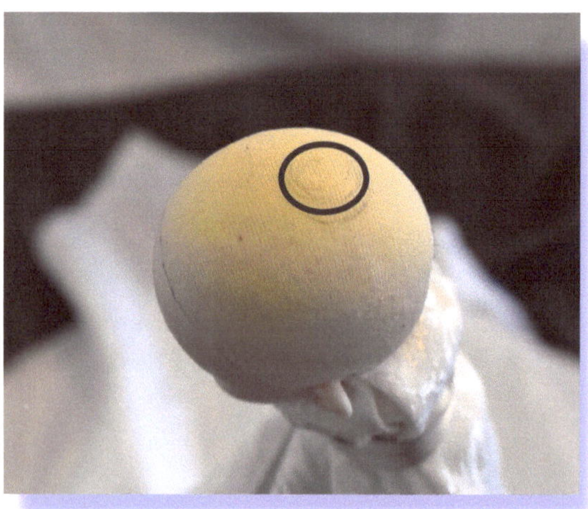

Above: This wig will be a "little boy" style wig, so therefore I have drawn a circle on the back of the head where boyish hairstyles are often parted.

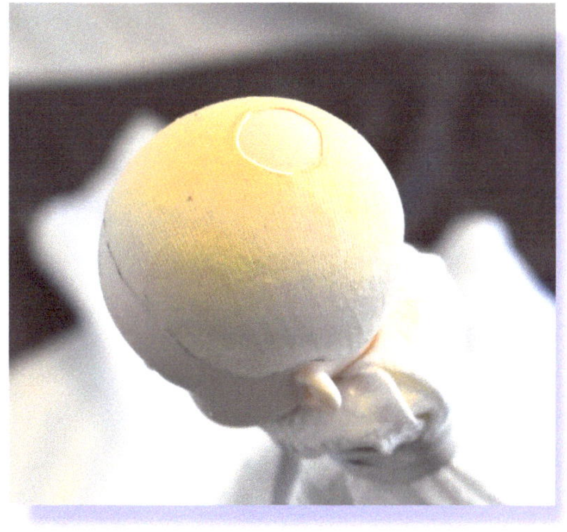

Now remove the wig cap and cut out the area you marked off for the hair part. Your wig cap now has a hole or is missing the entire front like a bald man.

Cover the doll's head in plastic wrap again. Brush some glue upon the doll's head where the hair part will be and, while the glue is still wet, place a piece of tulle over the glue.

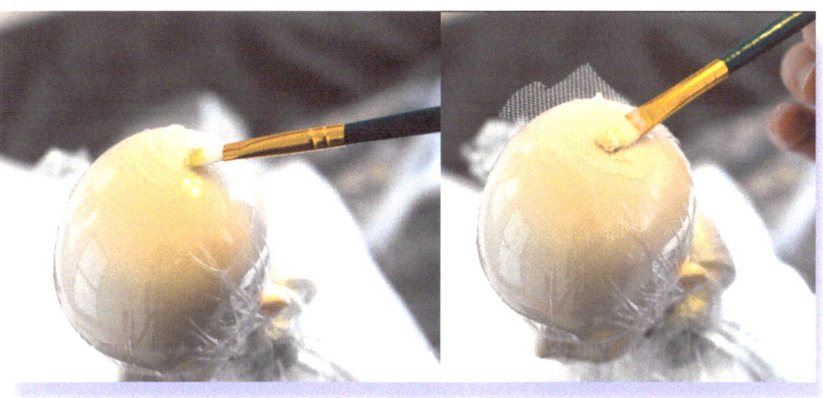

Now over the tulle, place the wig cap in the proper way it should sit. You should be able to see the tulle in the window you cut previously.

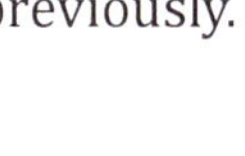

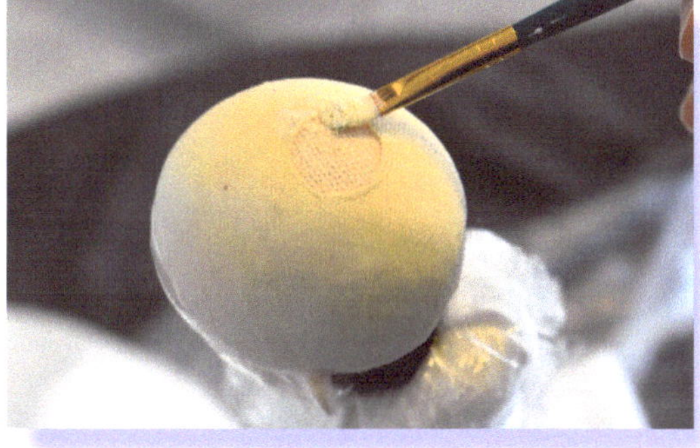

Over the wig cap opening, place another piece of tulle and glue it down, saturating both pieces of tulle and securing it to the wig cap. Make the top layer of tulle look neat; it should not cover the whole head, just enough to overlap and grab hold of the wig cap. Once the glue is dry you can remove the wig cap.

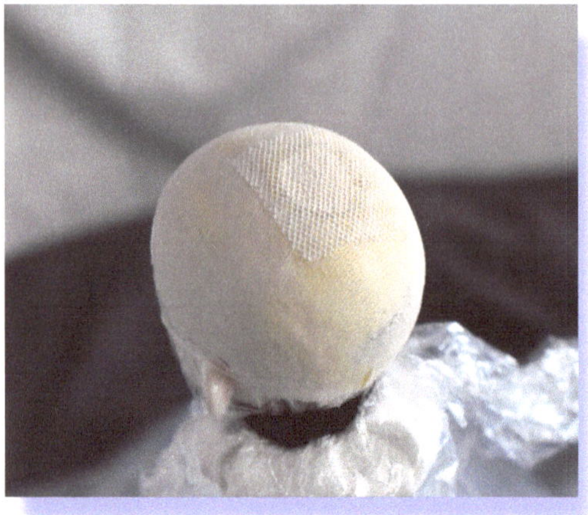

See what we did there? Now you are ready to attach the hair around the base via the **Gluing Technique** and then use the **Rooting Technique** when you get to the tulle window. If you didn't know which technique to use, why not use both? It's speedy to fill in most of the wig with glued hair and then realistic-looking at the rooted part. Even if you decide not to root once you get to the tulle, don't worry, you did not waste anything. Just keep on gluing like before. This is why mistakes don't matter very much in this craft.

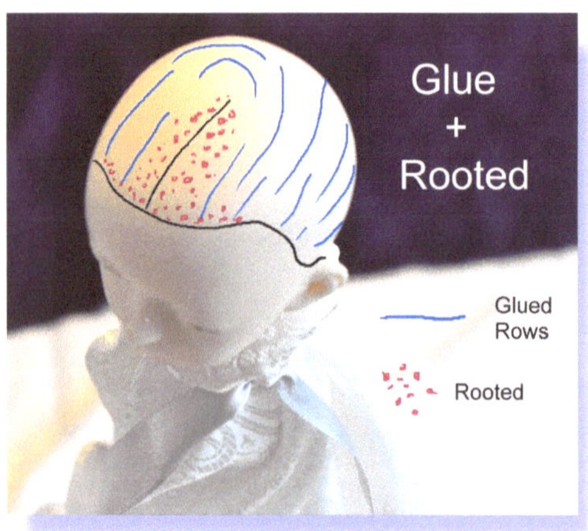

A Little Flocking Thrown in?

With the wonder of **Rooted** and **Punched** hair techniques, windows of opportunity will *whoosh* right open. Does your doll have a Mohawk or half his head shaved? Well before you root (or punch) hair into the wig cap, draw a line on the wig cap marking where exactly the hair should be and where the flocking will go. Add the hair and then brush or band it aside. Flocking is like the glue and glitter technique we learned in early grade school. Just cover the flocking area with your glue of choice, and then sprinkle your flocking (tiny bits of hair you cut beforehand) onto the glue until it is covered completely. Let dry and see how it looks.

Note: even if you are not interested in flocking, think about it anyway. Flocking may be a good way to cover the raw edge of an exposed wig cap once the wig is complete.

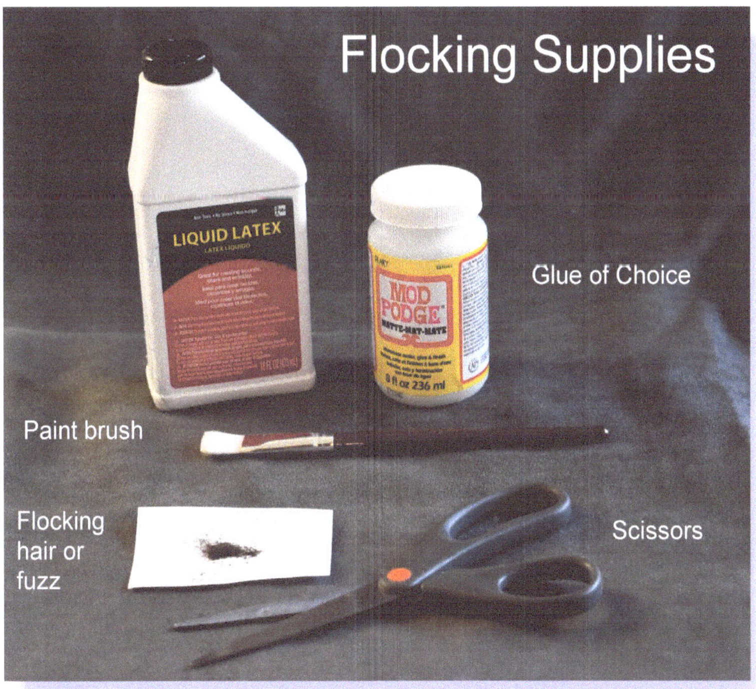

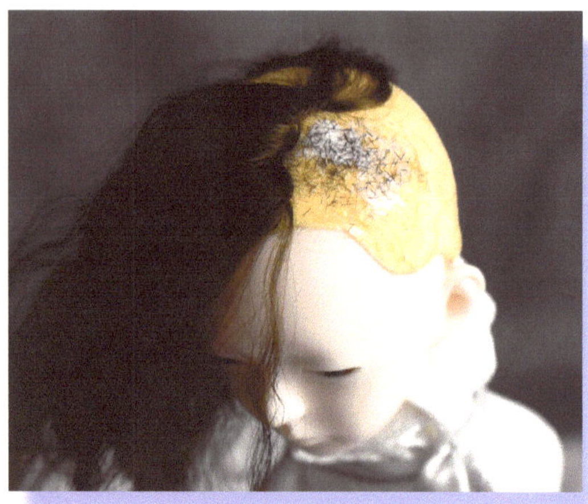

Above: The early stage of "flocking."

Glue + Rooting: My Own Journey to Improve D's Wig

"D" is my blue-haired doll. His wig was the first one I made, and was very pleased. But as time passed, I wondered if I could do better. I love this doll so much I figured he was worth the money and trouble to try again. My issue with D's wig is that, though beautiful and vibrant, it feels kind of… *big* around the top. It's a nagging feeling like his "hair dome" is not in very good proportion to the size of his face. So I want to make his next wig look "skinny." I want the top-most plane of his hair to lie closer to the plane of his actual head. It took a lot of hair to cover his entire **Rooted** wig, and so I feel I must use less hair to cover the same size wig. Let's see if I can pull it off!

Here is D's original wig. See how big the dome of his hair looks in comparison to the size of his face? I want to make a wig that sits less high and spans less wide at the sides.

Special Hair line

I'm drawing a special hair line for a certain effect of D's wig. I want his hair to be part-able all the way to the back. So I drew a thick hair line from front to back, sanctioning off the area that will be **Rooted**. The sides of the wig will be glued.

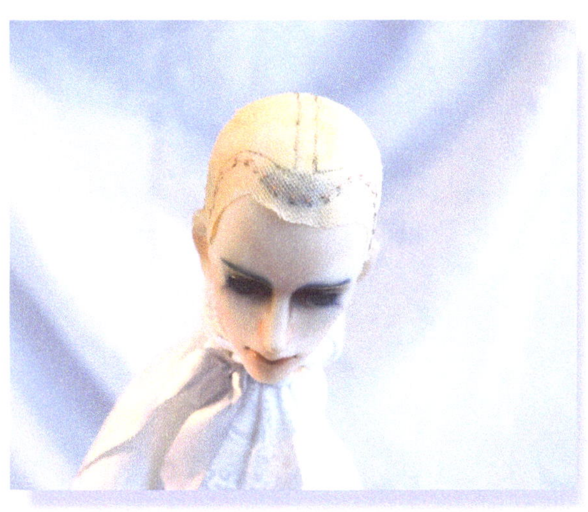

Hair Façade

Since I'm trying to use less hair to cover the same distance of wig cap, I'm going to cover the wig cap in a special coat of wool roving before attaching the alpaca hair. Wool roving is used mainly for yarn spinning, wet felting, and needle felting. Some people use it to make wigs too. It's particularly good for mohawks that stand on end. I'm just going to use it to cover up the baldness of the wig cap. This way, hopefully, I can use thinner locks, distance them farther apart than I otherwise would have, and avoid bald spots showing in the finished wig.

First, cover the doll head in plastic and put the wig cap on it. Make sure the parts of the wig cap that will need the wool roving are clearly marked. I still want the wig cap to show at the area where I will most likely part the hair.

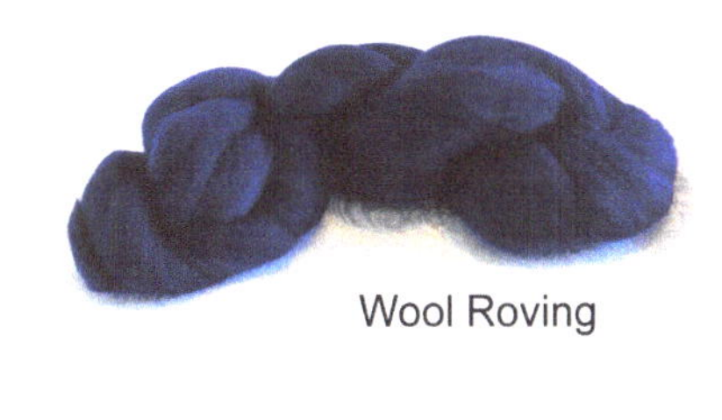
Wool Roving

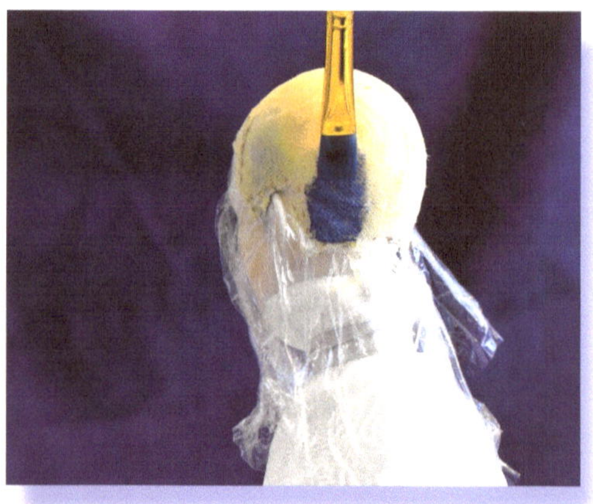

Next apply a thin, but good, layer of liquid latex to the sections that need wool roving. Just do small manageable sections at a time. I added blue paint to my liquid latex to help get an even blue façade throughout.

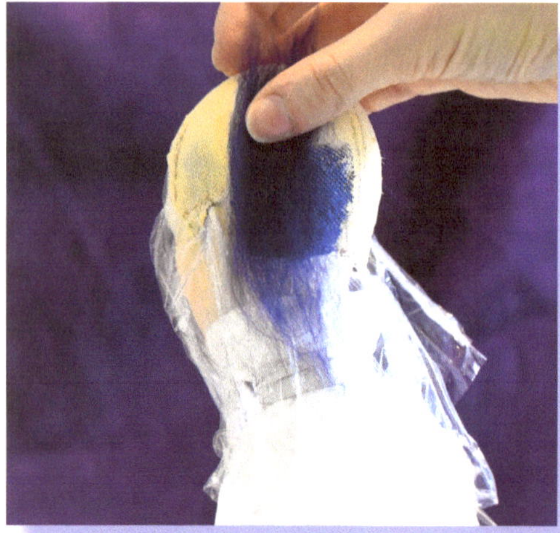

I prepared a THIN lock of wool roving, flattened it out, and laid it over the wet liquid latex. I use my fingers to dab it down as much as I can. I want this façade to feel and look like hair as much as possible so I did not brush more latex over the hair, I wanted it to retain its fuzzy texture.

Note: wool roving would be a very good material to cover up raw wig cap edges if needed, considering you have a color close enough to the hair color.

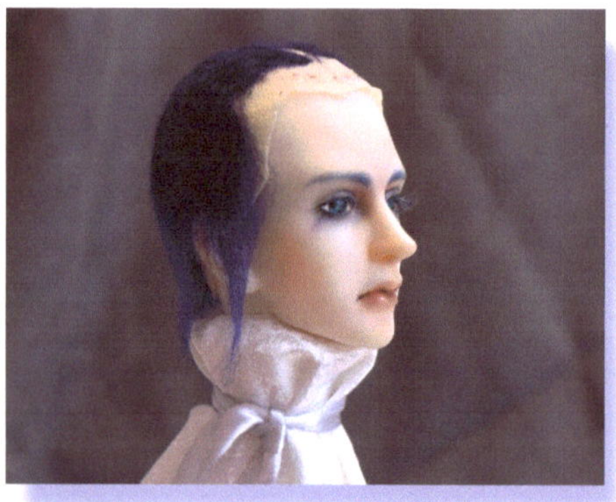

After it dried, I pulled the loose wool roving strands away and the wool that was tightly secured down remained. Next, I proceeded to glue my rows of hair down over the wool roving like in the **Gluing Technique**.

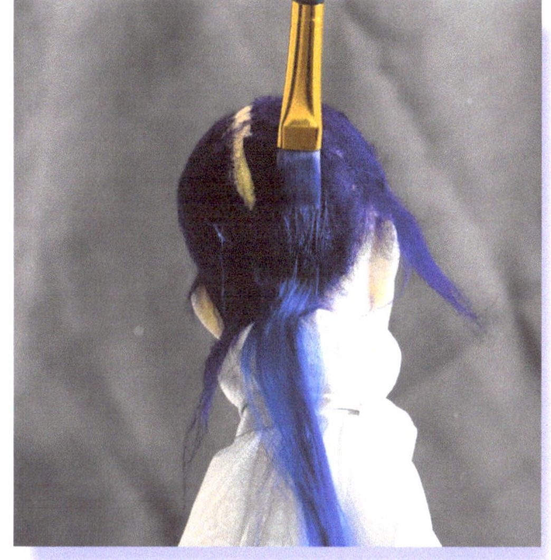

When I'm done, the wig has a strange bald spot. This area will be filled in by the **Punching** technique (later replaced with the **Rooting** technique).

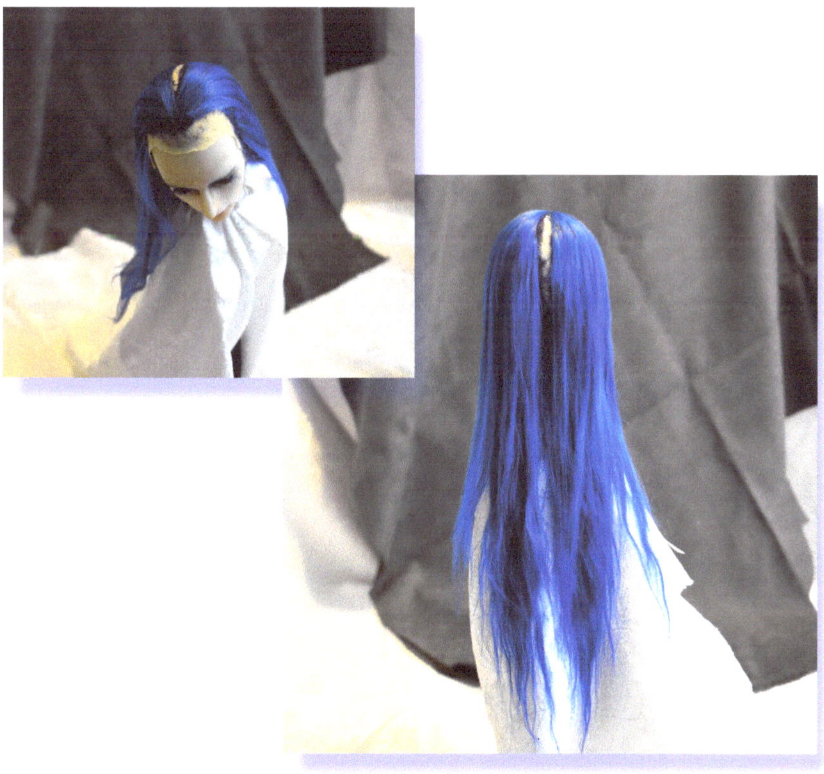

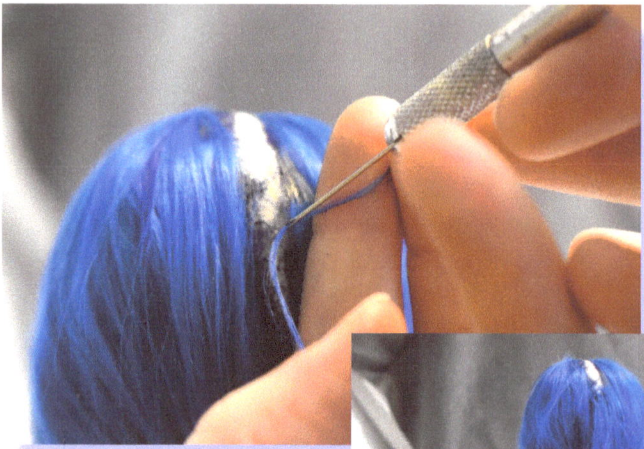

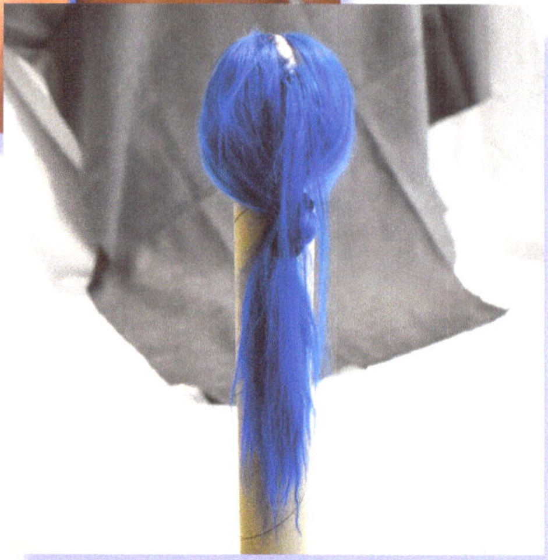

Additional Maneuver: Wig Cap Extension

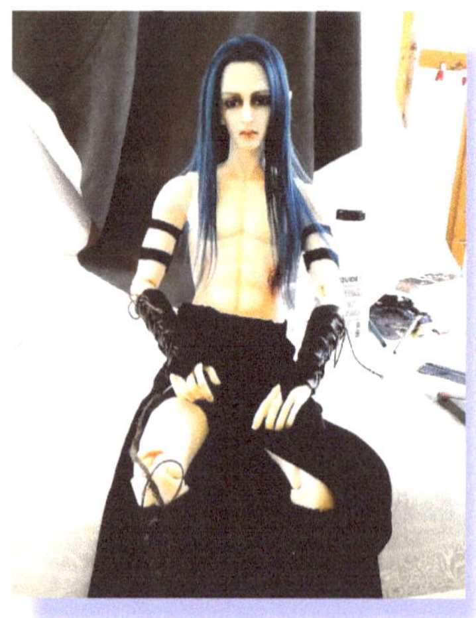

Above, you see the semi-final image of D's new wig that I took with my cell phone and posted online. Except there's one problem: his hairline may be too high! But it's ok, because I still have some hair and wig cap making materials left and it's never too late to make adjustments to the wig. Nothing has to be final. This is the main message I want to put across in this section. I want to show you that I, and everyone else, have frustrations and that nearly everything is fixable. One thing about this photo is that it may not be very obvious that there is a problem. To some people perhaps there's no problem at all. And it took me a while to decide if it was a problem or not. The photo looks good to me, but once I put him back into my doll cabinet, I noticed the problem: he just wasn't himself. He needed more work. The solution to this problem was extending the wig cap so that his forehead would not look quite so big. It's actually an easy thing to do, it just takes a little time.

Set the doll head up just like always! This time I slathered a good layer of glue right over his forehead (over the plastic wrap).

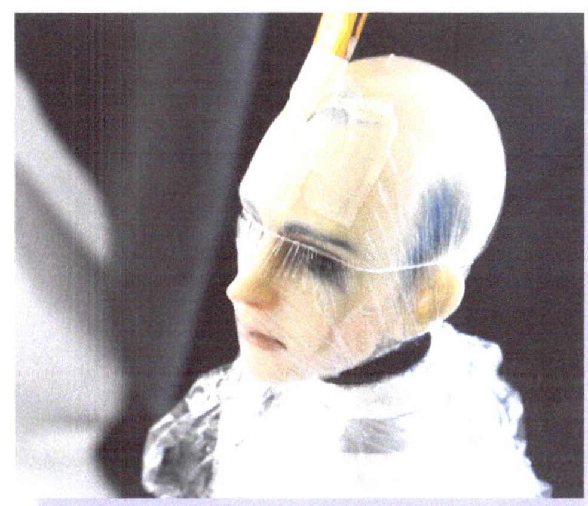

Note: You'll notice in the photos that I have two heads for my "D" doll. One of them has modified elf ears and the other does not. I'm taking advantage of this situation to use the incomplete head for all this wear-and-tear activity. I thought this was important to mention because later you will see his elf ears poking through the hair. Also, having a spare head of the same type may save the "good" head from potential damage.

Next, layer some tulle over the area where you painted the glue just like in the original **Tulle Wig Cap** technique. I recommend

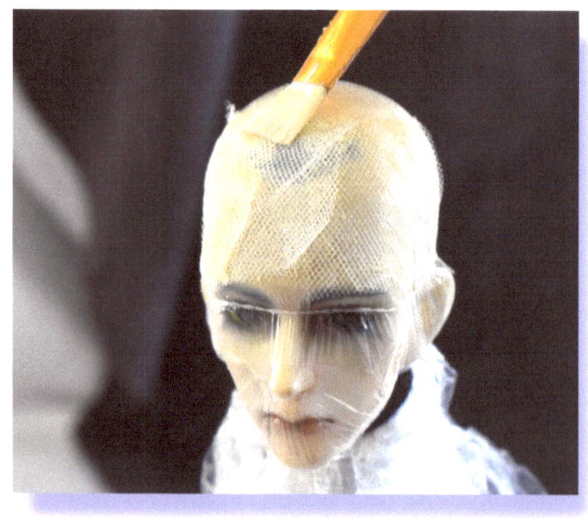

using tulle regardless of the type of wig cap you have already made. It is possible to hybrid them in this way. You only need to apply tulle to the area of the head where the wig cap will be extended, but be generous. You want to have MORE added area than needed, and you need the extension to overlap the area where the original wig cap already sits. Let the tulle dry before the next step so that it will be stronger to work with.

The next step is to slather more glue on top of it. While the glue is wet, carefully place the (ponytailed) wig on the doll's head, where it naturally sits, and over the glue and new tulle.

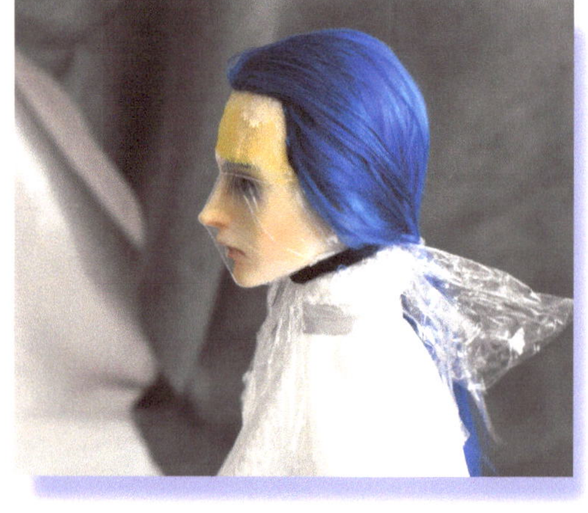

Press the wig down firmly over the glue to make sure they bond together. You can use your paintbrush to pack more glue into the front wig cap edges to make sure they bond together with very little chance of an opening forming.

Note: liquid latex is fabulous for this job because it tends to stick and bond very quickly. If you feel the need, you can band or tie the wig down firmly to the doll head to apply pressure while it dries.

Now let it dry for a long time.

Next you will draw the new hairline on the new tulle.

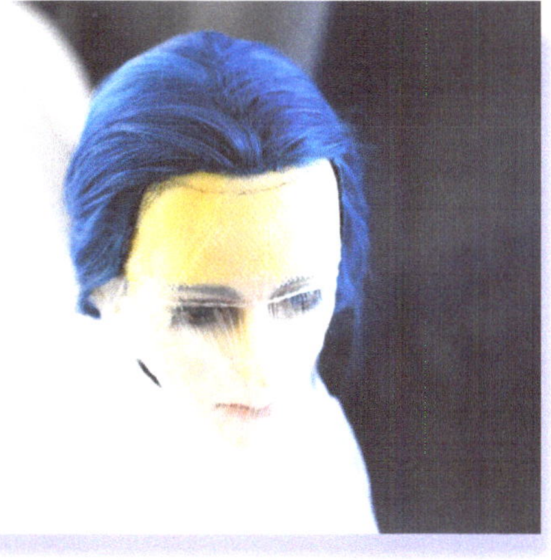

Remember that you probably don't need to add a huge amount of new space. Draw the new hairline where you would consider the ideal placement to be. But remember to still cut out MORE than the line you drew. You can always clip off the excess later and this also applies to the event that you may attach more hair than needed and want to get rid of it.

After drawing the new hairline, you can remove the wig from the plastic.

My new hairline looks a little distressed after peeling it away from the plastic. Don't lose heart if your extension looks like this, just keep working.

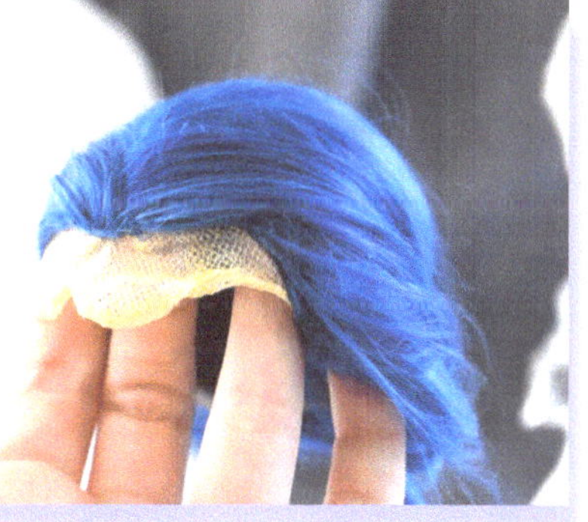

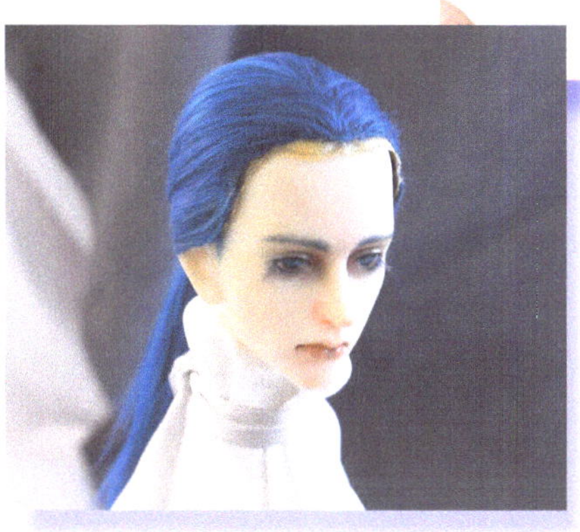

Here is my new hairline after clipping most of the excess tulle. As you can see it looks loose and is not laying flush to the doll's head. Once again, don't worry: we will be applying more glue to the inside and outside of it, causing it to become thicker, which results in a stronger structure.

Since this wig is not 100% **Rooted**, I decided to glue a bunch of extra hair down first to fill the space quickly. Later I will root the hair in at the center-front and wherever needed. Since this is the front, I needed to execute this as neatly as possible. And it was important that I mixed blue paint in with my liquid latex to improve the appearance. Otherwise the dried latex would have been very showy. The latex mixed with paint was less obvious.

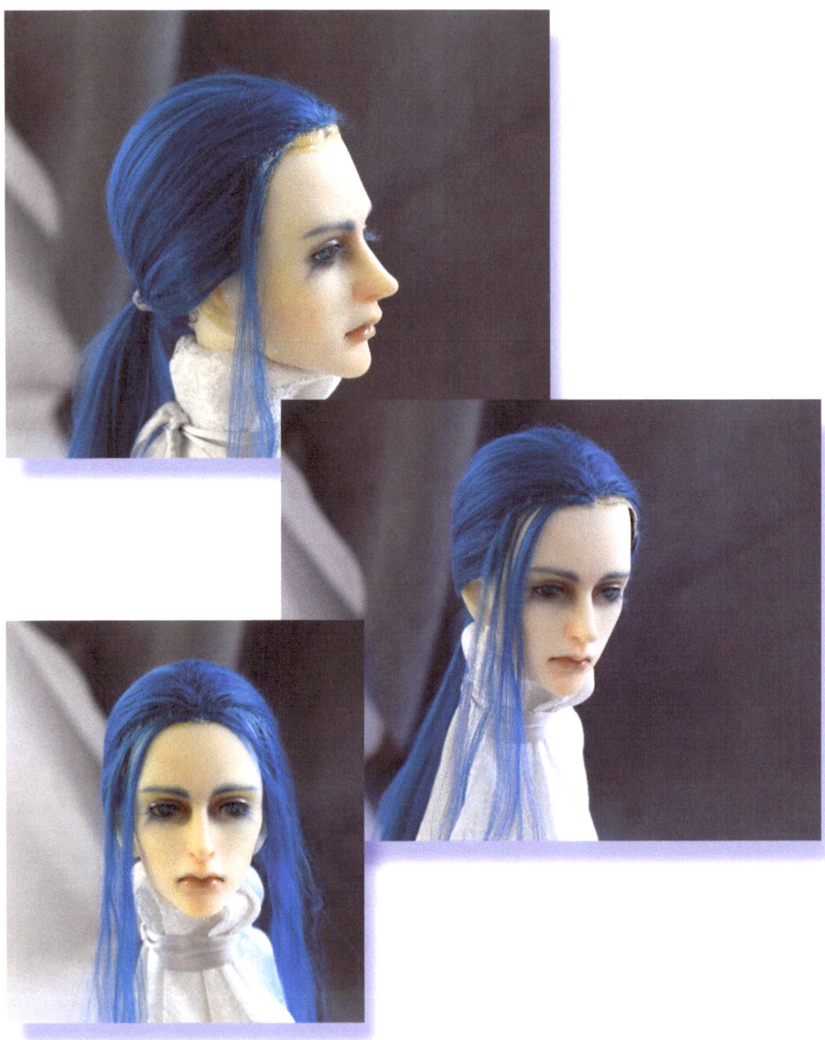

And the last step was to **Root** the finishing touches into the areas where the wig cap was showing or just to cover up the glued ends of the new hair. Below are some photos of the inside showing where the **Rooted** hair was added. It was also important to his final "look" to build up the hair thickly at the front-center for a full and realistic cascade.

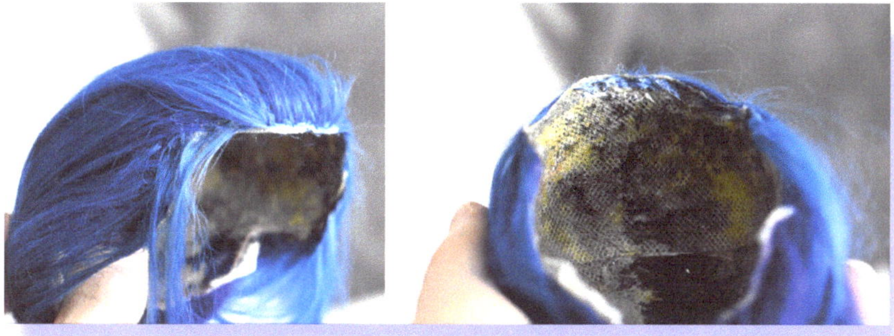

Above: Hair **Rooted** at the front and sealed with glue on the inside.

Now let's compare the new wig to the old!

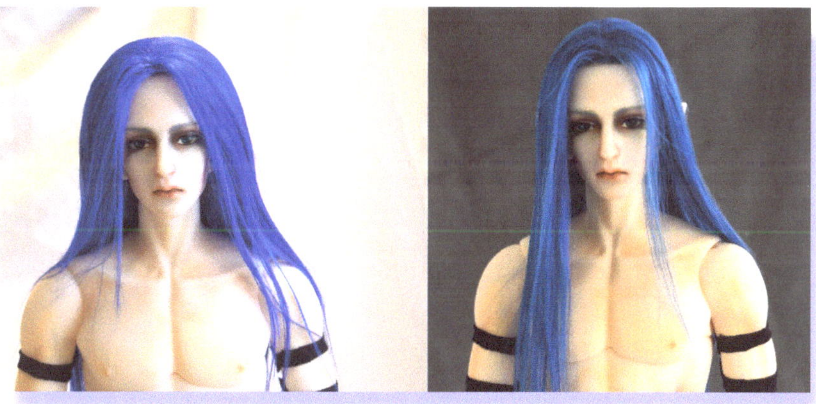

I like the new wig much better. It took far less alpaca hair to complete, the color seems more natural (by my opinion) after using the same blue dye to color light brown hair instead of pure white, and it achieved the thinner dome I was looking for. Notice that his pointy ears can be seen this time.

Chapter 9

Finishing Up

How you finish the wig depends on you. As one basic rule, you will probably comb the part into the hair wherever you want it and then use your curling or straightening iron to press the hair down flat. I personally prefer the straightening iron because mine seems hotter than my curling iron and I can chomp it down onto the wig for a good press (the heat does not damage the underside of the wig cap—just don't leave it there too long).

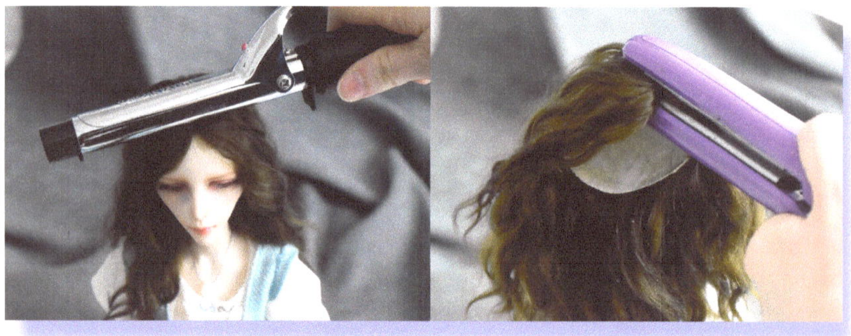

The Raw Wig Cap Edge

This can be dealt with in a few ways and one of them is to do nothing. Nothing is what I do to the edges when I've **Rooted** a wig. The long hair seems to cover it well and even if it's exposed, it seems pretty well camouflaged in the hair, particularly if you matched the tulle color to the doll color well. Using paint in the color of the hair has also worked for me in disguising the wig cap edge. I once used white thread to reinforce the edge of the wig cap and regretted it later. But as I've said before, it's never over, mistakes are usually fixable. So I painted over the thread using my paint color mixed with glue. Yes you can blend white glue and liquid latex with acrylic paint with no adverse effects. Just be careful not to mat the hair up in the glue-paint. This worked and my doll is enjoying that wig to this day.

The other way to finish off or disguise the wig cap's edge is to fold some hair from the front to underneath the wig cap and glue it down. This wraps the edge in hair to make it less obvious.

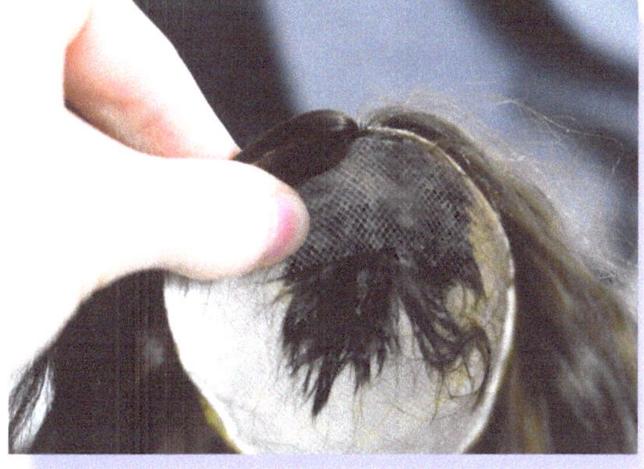

You can also go the opposite direction and glue some hair to the inside edges, fold to the outside, and iron down.

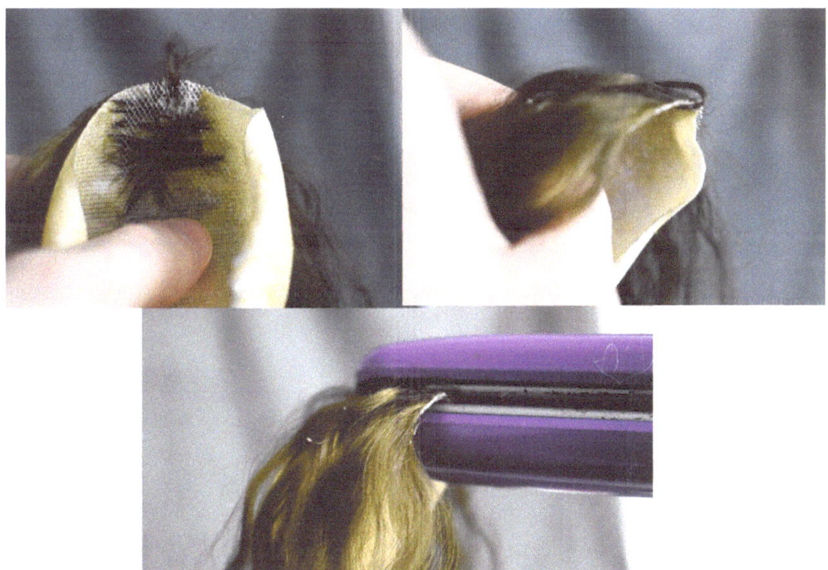

I've had trouble making the hair stay in this way. This may be a better option if you are going for a "slick back" look and all the hair is pointed backward. You may need to use a little glue to help it stay. Otherwise, if the hair has an average middle part then the hair will most likely fall to the sides and, hopefully, shield the edge of the wig cap anyway.

Or as I mentioned in the previous chapter, you can use flocking to cover the raw edge. This means snipping tiny bits of hair into a container, covering the raw edge with glue, and then sprinkling the hair bits over the glue and let dry.

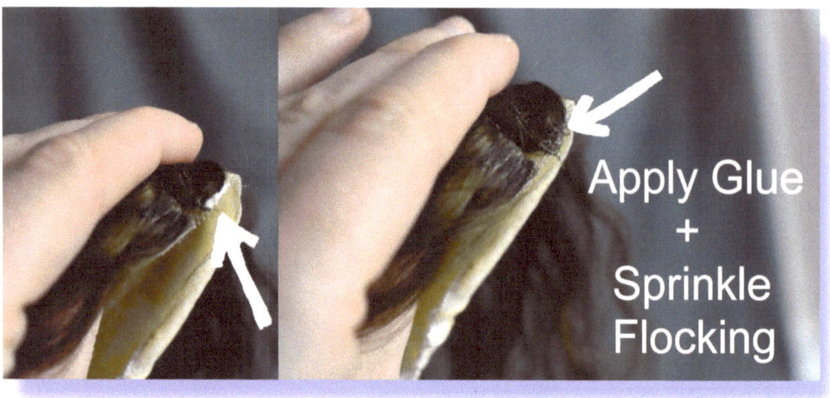

One Last Comb

Go ahead, you've earned it! After fiddling with the front edge of the wig cap you will probably need one last straightening with an oiled comb to finish off the brand new wig.

Note: When I did an Angora wig for Lamraen, I wanted to keep the hair's natural curls. I did not want to comb through and loosen them up. So I was very careful with the locks as I worked, using the **Gluing Technique**, and at the end did NOT comb through. I put some oil into the hair with my hands instead. Eventually I fear it will need combing for upkeep so I expect I will comb it and then wet it down thoroughly and let it air dry. Hopefully the curls will bounce back. I will also re-oil it with my hands. At the top of the next page is a photo of the two angora wigs. At left is uncombed and at right is combed.

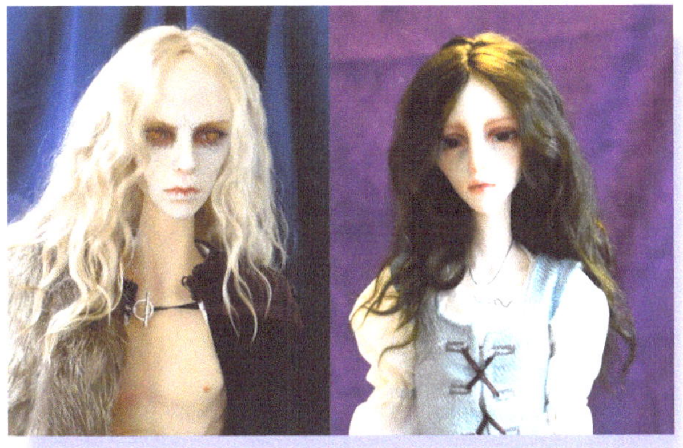

Parting and Re-parting the Rooted Wig

The fun thing about **Rooting** the whole wig is that you have total freedom to style it due to its free-growing nature. Try different parting angles to see how they look on your doll. But you have to be careful with alpaca hair as it is fine and wooly and will like to bond together. To re-part alpaca hair, begin to comb it lightly where the part is. Comb front to back and as the hair loosens up you can comb deeper, until all of the hair is going in the same direction.

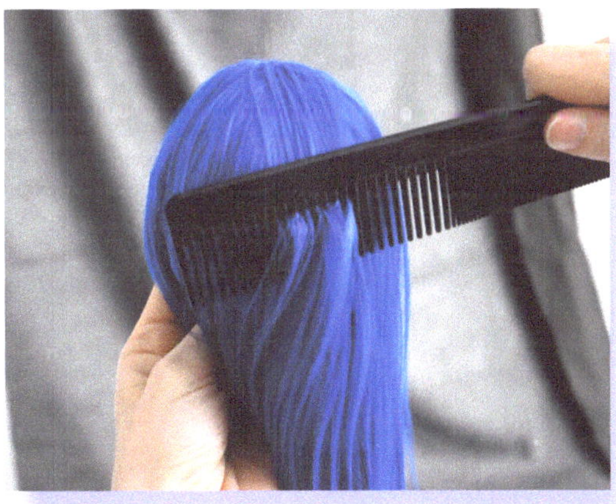

With the hair lying backward, it will be easy to divide into a new part somewhere else on the wig. You can also comb back to front or side to side for a funkier style.

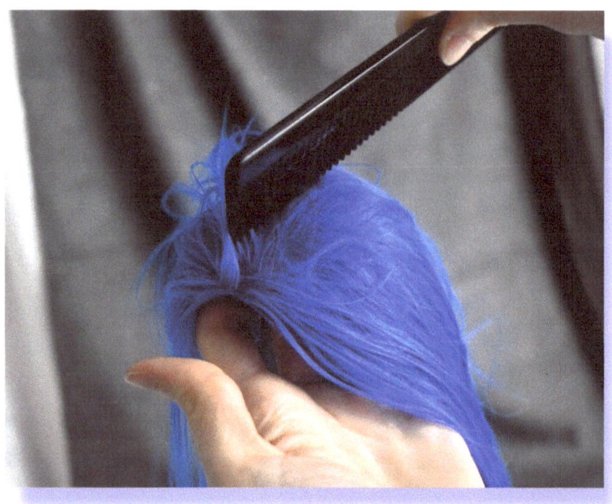

Cutting the Hair

Next you may want to trim and or layer the hair. Don't sweat it, I don't know a thing about cutting hair but I still manage and you can too. Get a good pair of scissors, something sharp and not decades old. You can now decide what the style will be, I just have a few examples and how-to's.

Straight Trim

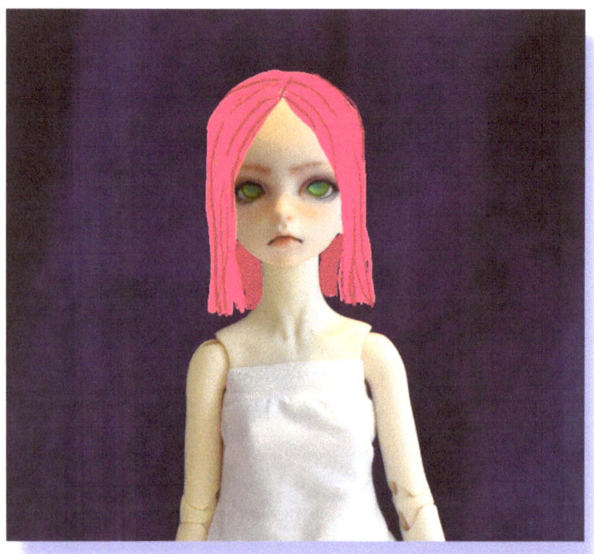

Not much explanation for this one. It is cut straight across—that's all you do. Just take your time and stay focused. It may help to hold the hair between two fingers. And if there are any jumps and dips in the line of hair ends then carefully trim them away until the edge is even. Go slow and leave a generous amount at first, you can always cut a little more, but you can't go back once the hair is cut.

Bangs

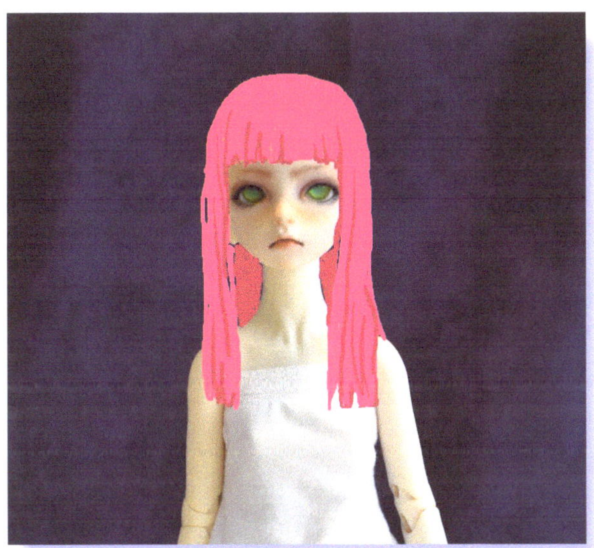

Bangs are probably easier achieved with the **Rooting** or hybrid technique. To make bangs on one of these wigs, simply brush the front hair forward over the doll's eyes. This only needs to be a thin curtain of hair. You may need to apply heat to make the bangs stay in this new direction. Then trim across according to the desired length.

The Jagged Trim

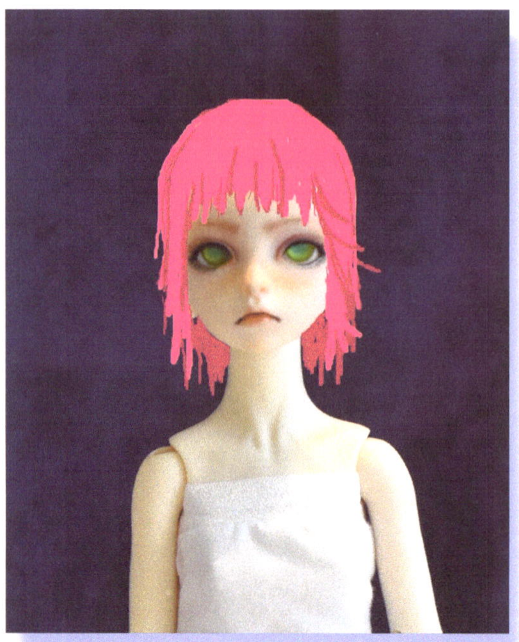

This can be applied to the above two hairstyles. Cut across as you did before but this time cut it LONGER than you actually want. You need room to trim the jags into it. Now turn your scissors vertical, parallel to the hair, and begin snipping at the tips of the hair in this manner until you've achieved the organic shape, texture, and length you want.

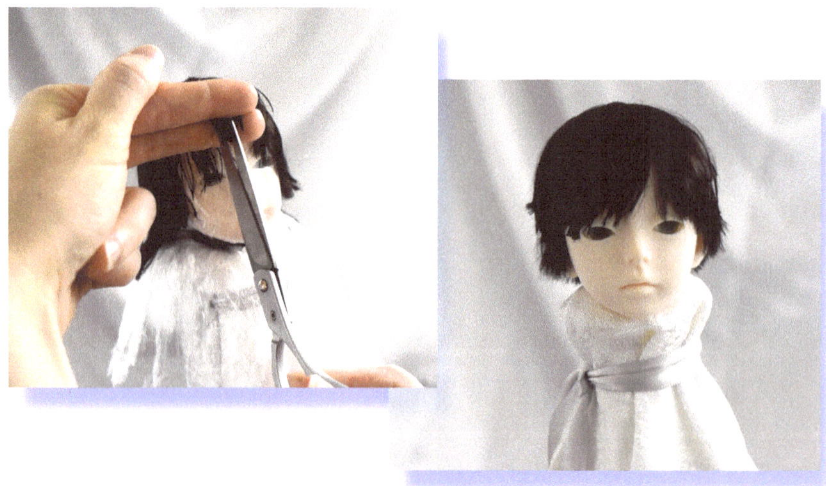

Layers

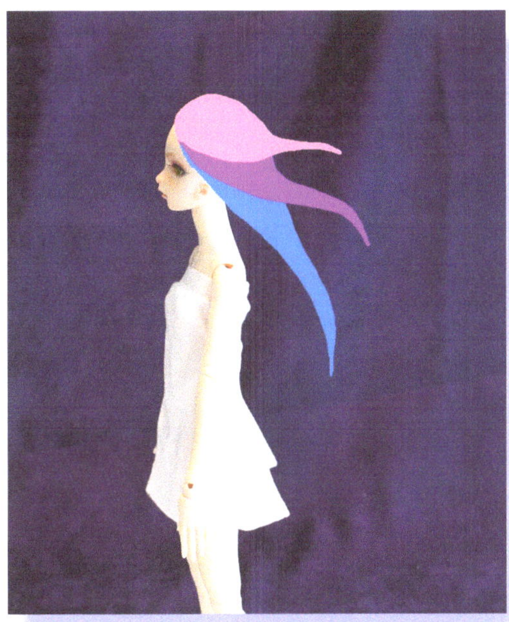

Imagine that the hair is divided into sections, bottom, middle, and top, and will be arranged also as long, medium, and short. The long layer is at the bottom of the wig and underneath the shorter layers.

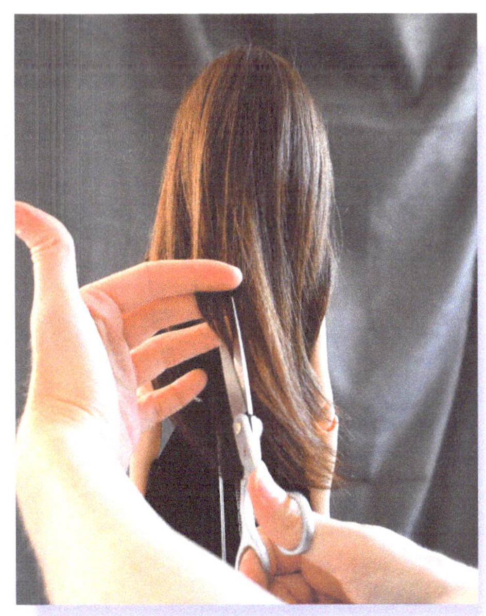

Tend to the long/bottom layer first by trimming it to your desired length, and or applying the **Jagged** look mentioned above. When the overall length and texture looks good, move up to the next tier. You'll need to separate the next layer from the bottom layer to work on it so that the bottom layer does not get tampered with anymore. You can either use your fingers or a stick to separate the layers. Unless you want to trim it straight across (like the "hime cut"), you will need to cut each layer using the **Jagged** method mentioned above. Cut it with the scissors held vertically and parallel to the hair.

When you drop the layer it should have a natural organic texture as it sits upon the previous layer. It may also blend in. Do this for as many layers as you think the wig should have—it may have three and it may have ten. As you arrive to the front, you will need to decide how long the top and front-most layer hangs. It may be as long as the jawline, ear, shoulders, etc. Either way, cutting it while the doll is wearing it is recommended. You can use the doll's body parts as landmarks for the various layers.

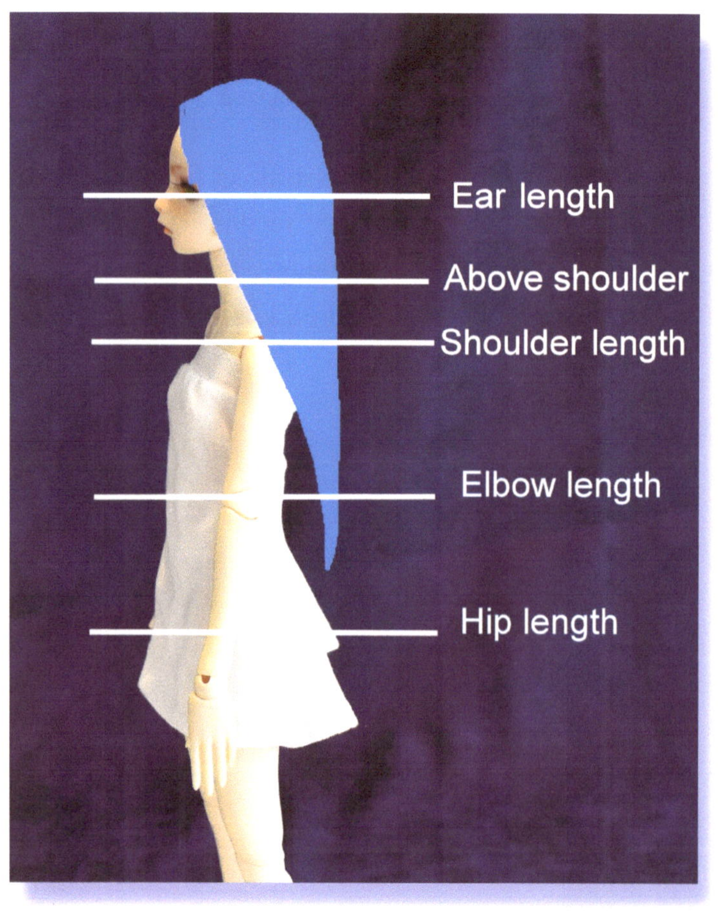

Problems with the Fit

Sometimes when a wig is finished we may notice that the wig cap shrank or warped and no longer seems to fit properly. If this is the case for you, do not panic. Commonly for me, when I make **Rooted** wigs with a **Tulle Wig Cap**, they tend to warp and become too large for the doll's head. This was especially the case for the first blue wig I made, it took a lot of abuse during creation and seemed loose upon completion. I fixed it by determining where the looseness was happening and applying a little hot glue in that area. The hot glue is lumpy and can fill in the "empty" spots of the wig cap as well as act as a grip so that the wig cap doesn't slide or fall off. I think added hot glue lines or dots may also work well with any wig that is too big or too slippery.

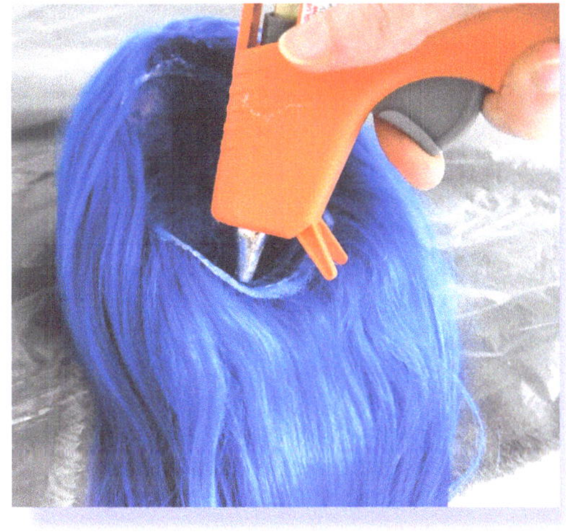

There is something on the market called "silicone wig caps" which are little caps meant to be worn under the wig to add friction so that the wig doesn't slide. You can buy them for a very small price. One downside is that sometimes the doll's head measurement doesn't exactly match the standard sizes for the silicone wig caps. Therefore some people have found ways to think outside the box. Another very good under-cap can be made from a common balloon. This one is my favorite and generally all of my dolls use one. Just cut off the "neck" of the balloon and use the rounded part as the cap. The neck itself is good for tiny dolls. You may have to track down jumbo-sized balloons if you have a doll with a head larger than ten inches in circumference.

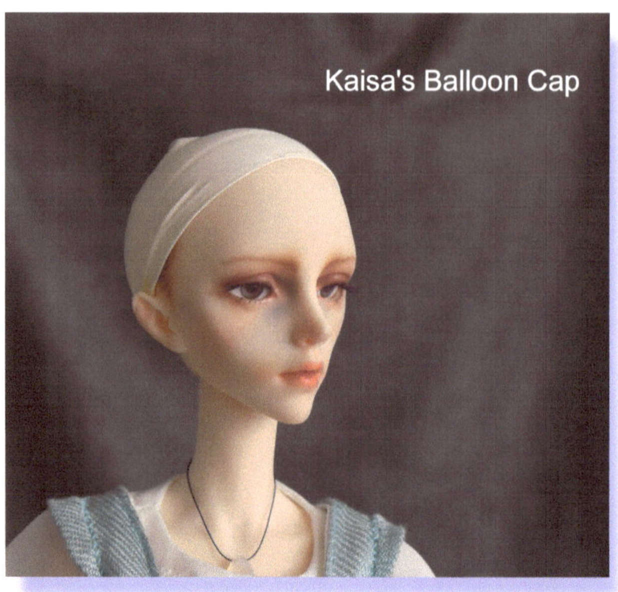

Does the wig seem too small? Perhaps it shrank after all the gluing and the edges seem to have receded. This is a common problem for me! A balloon under-cap may help in holding the wig in place, but sometimes this wig's lack of surface space can look unattractive.

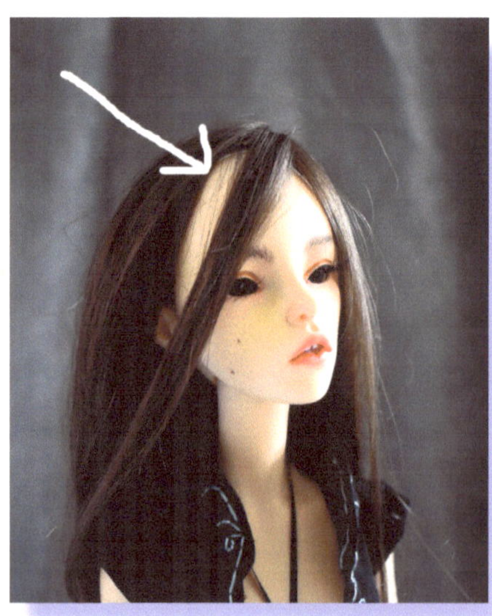

At left: If the wig cap is too small, the hair may struggle to cover the necessary parts of the head. A wig cap extension may be needed.

Perhaps when the hair moves a certain way the doll looks bald underneath. The best way I know to fix this problem is to drag all my wig-making supplies out again and go to the trouble of extending the wig cap. I won't say that this is hard, but it's definitely not the fastest, easiest fix either. It means going back to the work table and continuing working on the wig basically. You will be creating a little more wig cap and gluing/rooting more hair. You may have thought the wig was done but now it's a bummer to have to continue. But don't despair because it will be worth it, especially after all that time you spent on the wig already. Don't give up now when you are so close! Refer back to Chapter 8: Additional Maneuver: Wig Cap Extension to find out how to do this.

Frequently Asked Questions

The following are real questions I received online about doll wig-making.

Money Questions

Q: How much did it cost you to make a wig?

A: This varies greatly! But the basic quote I would say is $80-$100. This is, of course, for using the techniques in this book with natural animal hair. The first wig I made cost the most (at LEAST $80) because I had to buy oddball things like a bottle of mineral oil and a hair straightening iron. If you already have a hair straightening iron you are that much ahead. But now that I have these things, they last a long time and the next few wigs will be considerably cheaper. A 4 oz. bottle of liquid latex will last for several wigs, so you can rest easy knowing that this big $100 shopping list is actually good for several wigs. But the hair is something you will probably renew for each wig, and my last hair purchase cost approximately $61.50 after shipping.

Q: Are these the wigs I keep seeing online for $100+?

A: Basically yes! But if you read the question before this one then hopefully you can forgive those Etsy sellers who are trying very hard to make a living doing what they love doing! The Suri Alpaca hair tends to be very expensive and it can take a good 8 hours or more to craft a **Glued Wig** (30+ hours for a hand-sewn **Rooted** wig). Please remember you are buying more than the materials, you are buying someone's hard work and time. Buying a wig will save YOU precious time and effort, though making a wig comes with its own rewards. The good news is that I found these fabulous hand-crafted wigs to be made very simply, using nothing more than the techniques found in this book and therefore you too can save a little money by creating your own—especially if you have multiple dolls!

Q: Where do you buy the hair?

A: I buy mine exclusively on Etsy.com. It is available elsewhere, like on Ebay, but I find Etsy to be more doll-savvy and offer more options for hair types, length, colors, washed, unwashed, etc.

Materials Questions

Q: How much alpaca fiber did you use?

A: I make wigs mostly for dolls with an 8 and ½ inch head circumference—they are considered to be 1/3, 70cm, or SD (Super Dollfie) size. And when I made the first alpaca wig, I estimated that I used half of the 3 ounces I bought, therefore, I used 1 and ½ ounces. But I would recommend getting at least 2 ounces for a doll of this size. I always buy 3 ounces! Keep in mind that you will be combing a lot of "junk hair" out of it. If you are buying a different type of fiber or working on a different sized doll, then I strongly urge you to do heavy research over the net for information from folk who have made wigs for similar dolls to yours. Research is just part of this hobby!

Q: What kind of dye should I use for faux fur?

A: Since faux fur is technically considered a fabric then I would try fabric dye—especially one made for synthetics, because faux fur is not real fur.

Q: What kind of oil do you use to comb the hair and why?

A: I use mineral oil to condition my alpaca hair (and sometimes angora hair) while I comb it. I noticed first off when I started working with alpaca hair that it was full of static which worsened when I tried to comb it. Animals have a natural oil (called lanolin for sheep) that conditions their hair naturally. And it was told to me that keepers of alpacas and other show animals will use mineral oil to comb the hair to make it look glossy and luxurious just before a competition. So therefore that is what I use to comb the cut alpaca hair. Since it was cut, it no longer gets its natural oil from the animal's body and will dry out pretty bad when washed with detergent. Each step explained in this book, from washing to conditioning, to combing/oiling, and then ironing puts the hair through a process that transforms it into beautiful.

Q: Is that a special kind of latex?

A: As far as I know there are two kinds of latex: that used to make big props and masks, and that used for makeup effects. The one used for makeup effects is gentler on human skin especially for people who are allergic to latex. If you are allergic to latex, you may want to do some research to find out if it's ok for you to use this for crafting. The makeup kind is fine for wigs—it's what I use. You can look for it anywhere special effects makeup is sold, particularly at seasonal Halloween stores. I just order mine on Ebay, usually in 4oz bottles.

Q: Doesn't the latex smell awful?

A: It smells a little weird but no. It is not noxious and will not harm your lungs or your pets' lungs. You can use it indoors.

Q: Does it smell bad when it dries?

A: It smells even less bad when dry. It smells like a rubber band because it is rubber, but to tell the truth, I think it smells LESS intense than a rubber band.

Q: But doesn't the latex turn yellow?

A: Basically yes. Ordinary flesh tone latex even looks a bit yellow as soon as it dries and it may turn yellow in a matter of years or less depending on whether your latex object has been in the sun a lot. But I still love latex and plan to use it always. One way to compensate for the yellowing may be to add paint to it in the color of your doll's "skin." I have not tried this and none of my wigs are a year old yet, so I can't guarantee anything, but a good quality acrylic paint may help to hold the color if you are worried about this. I am not worried, so I don't use paint unless I'm trying to disguise the wig cap edges in some way. I basically just cover the wig cap where necessary. I'm sure I won't mind if a little of the yellow wig cap shows at the top where the hair is parted.

Technique Questions

Q: Can you reroot using liquid latex?

A: Tough question. I'm assuming you mean to reroot a Barbie doll's head—sealing the hair on the inside with latex? My answer would be maybe. I think if you do that then it may be hard to dismantle for a future reroot. If the question is geared toward using the **Rooted Technique** in this book, then it is possible to a degree. I think sealing it on the inside with latex would create too much of a buildup and the cap would no longer fit on the doll's head when finished. But I did manage this by combining both **Gluing** and **Rooting** techniques into one wig.

Q: Would the traditional wig making technique using a net cap and tiny bent "crochet" hook tool they use to knot the hairs into it work for dolls?

A: I think yes. Seems like any technique scaled down to doll size would work. As long as you can manage to make the proper kind of net wig cap in that size then I think it would be very possible to knot hairs into it in the traditional way. I would love to see someone do this and even try it for myself!

Washing Questions

Q: I heard that using hot water to wash wool will felt/mat the hair. Do I have to use cold water?

A: Technically hot soapy water and agitation is how felt is made. If you just make the water slightly warm then the hair will be ok, you can also use cold if you want. It's also important not to rub the hair with your fingers, just swish it through the water to prevent knots. I don't like using cold water because it freezes my hands and I want to be comfortable for this long process.

About the Author

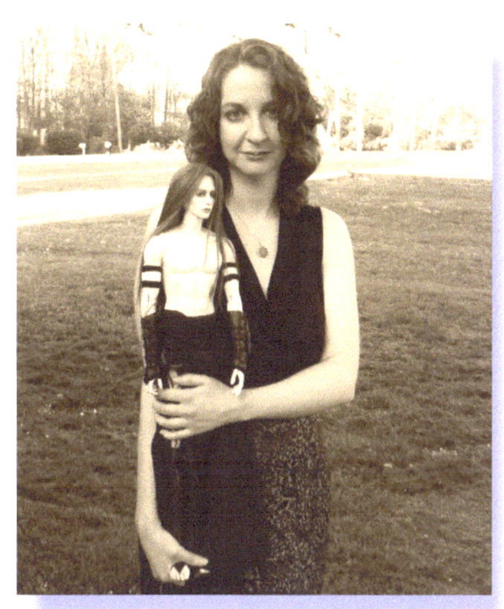

I am an artist basically. I took college art classes for about four years and experienced a sort of creative enlightenment. I found out that there are many ways to make something happen, and learned about actual tools and mediums which help bring a project out of my head and into the tangible world. It was this enlightenment that inspired me to write books to help you learn the same thing about yourself.

My main medium is oil painting for which I have won a number of awards in college and still like to exhibit around Nashville, Tennessee now and again. My favorite artists are the Dutch masters of the 1600's like Rembrandt and Vermeer. I'm developing my art style into what I consider "gothic revival," and the themes are devoted to the world of my own fantasy novels

I have also published *How to Rock at BJD Face-Up: A Beginner's guide to Painting Resin Doll Faces* to help beginners in the art of doll face painting. You can find it on Amazon, iBooks, Barnes & Noble, and most other major book sellers.

I am writing a variety of books! If you would like to check out my fiction and get the news of future craft books then please follow my social media pages listed below:

facebook.com/jchartcarverbooks

facebook.com/suffermist
instagram.com/suffer_mist
patreon.com/jchartcarver

Thank you so much for buying this book and all your support. Keep an eye out for my novels and future books about the wide and awesome world of doll customization! If you enjoyed this book then please consider leaving a review at your favorite retailer!

-Jesslyn Carver

Also available at most major retailers!

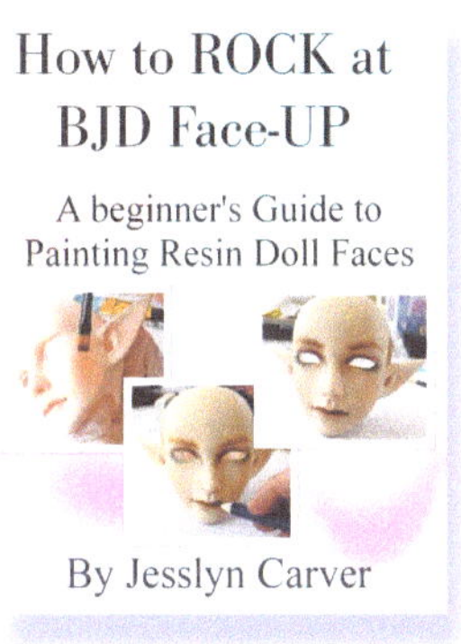

How to Rock at BJD Face-Up: A Beginner's Guide to Painting Resin Doll Faces

By Jesslyn Carver

www.ingramcontent.com/pod-product-compliance
Lightning Source LLC
LaVergne TN
LVHW052254100826
845147LV00001B/40

* 9 7 8 0 9 9 8 2 1 0 4 3 8 *